TOWARD LOVE

D.R. Wagner

Toward Love
& Selected Poems

D.R. WAGNER

Bottle of Smoke Press
North Salem, NY

FIRST EDITION

ISBN-13:   978-1-937073-76-3

Bottle of Smoke Press
29 Sugar Hill Road
North Salem, NY 10560

www.bospress.net

for

Annalesa Morlock (Wagner)
Gabrielle Wagner
Mikey West
John Dorsey
Stuart Walthall
E.R. Baxter III
Alice Anderson
T.L. Kryss

TABLE OF CONTENTS

TOWARD LOVE

WHERE THE STARS ARE KEPT.

1. A HANDFUL OF STARS

2. TWO LIES

3. GRACE

PRIVATE ARCHÆOLOGY

A LIMITED MEANS OF EXPRESSION

PROLOGUE:

1. LIMITED MEANS

4. THE PERFECT OFFERING

DIMENSIONS OFTHE MORNING

TOWARD LOVE

TOURNAMENT OF DREAMS

The walls were old wood.
Very old, like ships dragged
From the oceans centuries
After they sank.

The way your voice cracks
Through the post midnight
Air, thick with insect noises.
The gnawing at images
As soon as they are born.

"We're making a terrible
Mistake using dreams
Like this. There is a reason
Sleep has them as kingdoms."

Great birds hover over
Long dining tables. All is disarray.
Reckless as Winter.
Their language and voices
Belong to ogres, creatures with too many
Teeth in their mouths.

Battalions of faces without bodies,
Straight from the bonfires.
We come back with maps
Showing no place we could
Ever get to.

We can meet in dreams.
There will be tournaments
Of dreams. Come find us.

CLASH BY NIGHT

The armies had just begun
To work. The air strikes
Had been called in.
The bombardment had begun.

The wind was in the trees.
I was on my knees.
I found myself asking please.
Please, please stop the clowning.

I have broken everything in the room
And probably my own heart,
Certainly not yours.

I could see the light switchblade
On your sling back high heels
And watch the little fires
As you walked away, turn
Into tiny wings that made no sound.

A TALE

The room was empty.
One could hear heartbeats.
That was a good idea.
It kept anyone from speaking.

Our bodies began to lose their way.
We kept looking to the windows.
They were filled with faces of those
Who knew us at one time of our lives
And are now gone but haul themselves
Across our souls, trying to fit us to clothing
That was never our own. The confusion
Causes children to pour into the room.

"Give us this poem, fool." the voices say.
They sound like pixies and pull at my clothing.
"You have no idea where this poem will go.
It will push past you and whatever you might know."
A few of them bit at me, catching at bits of my soul.

I lifted the poem high in the air, close to my face.
I could see the room, still empty, but with a curious
Glow moving through it. The poem was still alive.
I could see our bodies floating toward the doors.

"We must leave this poem now. No good will come
Of it. It tells us only of confusion." I forced myself
To look up. The air began to fill with the most beautiful
Birds. They began to speak in their bird voices and I knew
We would be safe but that we must leave the poem
Immediately. I pulled the pixies from my clothing and skin.

I found the door partly ajar and squeezed through
The opening. The dawn was just arriving with its lamps
And the smell of food being cooked for a breakfast.
We hurried toward where voices were rising from
With the morning light. I can tell you no more.
Know this was not a dream.

RAINY EVENING

Slipped out, just inside the rain.
A window down the street was
Keeping quiet with its yellow
Light, surrounded by rain sounds,
Water dripping from the eaves,
Down my collar, shivering my mind.

There is not a soul on Key Street this evening.
Even the cats, who own the street, have found
Shelter away from cars and porches.
They have hidden themselves beneath
The old wooden houses here in Locke.
No one will ask for them. They have become
Rain spirits. The night and the streetlights
Own them. Gravel still crunches beneath
My shoes. I look for the door to my apartment.
Rain drips from the brim of my straw hat.

I find my way to my front door, climb the stairs.
I find a tumbler and fill it with ice and sake.
Looking out the window. Rain talking to the rooftop.

Thomas Merton, e.e. cummings, Kenneth Patchen,
Ingrid Swanberg, Melissa Studdard, Viola Weinberg,
Kent Taylor, E.R Baxter III, Henry Thoreau, Tom Kryss,
John Dorsey, Alice Anderson, Al Winans, Meg Pokrass,
Cassandra Dallett, Jorge Borges, Aliki Barnstone,
Italo Calvino, d.a. levy, raindrops of poets.
All against the window pane. Their voices on the rooftops,
Dripping into my breathing and my very soul.

THREE MEN CARRYING STONES

I met three men carrying stones.
"We have come to stop the tides.
Each day it disappears and then
Comes back, or sends its sons,
Small and great or its daughters,
Who make love to the moon and make
It too disappear. We will wait for no one."

I showed them the drowned cities,
Let them speak to the lost souls
Owned by nothing, not even time.

"Time is blind." they said.
Their voices were like bells
Sparkling below the stars.
"It has no substance. It can
Only pursue. It shows us only
Massive particles and tries
To explain creation as if it owned it."

I will tell you nothing more
My sweet friends of the horizon,
Until you sleep beside me
That we may know the awe
Of each others' breathing.

There will be other ways to say
These things. Perhaps birds
Know something we may never
Know and yet they speak of it
Constantly, acrobats of fireworks.

I have been standing in the cave
At the edge of the sea for days
Now. The stones are tossed
Into the ocean. They are of

Many sizes. Every question
I have asked these men has
Been answered by the most glorious
Gestures of their hands and their smiles.

BAD WATER

We didn't realize the rage of the river
Until we climbed to the high bank.
Looking down we saw the rapids
Going on and on as far as the eye could see.

Why this insistence to hurry back to the sea?
A nightmare where one holds on with fingertips
To what is left of one's mind while still
Being able to see shadows as belonging
To all other things but not to oneself.

A direction in the middle of the air.
An atrocious fabrication compounded
By perception and remembrances,
Not necessarily coming from ourselves.

Evening was very near. Even from this height
One could hear the great waterfall leaning
Over the edge of its precipice, cursing
With its language of horror and splendor.
Crashing into the rocks far below.

The river was the only way to proceed.
All else was endless plains, rainstorms
Boiling in the distance, purple clouds,
Lightning and the calls of frightened birds.

Every step we took elicited more questions.
Our memory became crystal, then dust and years.
Which is life. Which is dream. Which is death?

BREAKING THE SEAL

I always thought no one could
Touch me here where I
Was able to stand and speak this way.
It was a prayer.

I held a broken circle in my hand.
I would walk through the garden
Holding it as well as I was able.

I was never that delicate.
I could never control what
I imagined was true love.
This is it. I'm sure. Isn't it?

You became a flock of birds.
Swallows in the last light of day
Swirling and darting through my bloodstream.

BREAKING THE TRANCE

Born white, a cloud
And without vestments,
Able to kiss the raven.

All is bowing and the sunrise
Tightening the strings to invent
Perfect tones; the kind
The Pied Piper used
To deliver children
To the mountain's door.

The skin falls away
From the bones.
Burnt by the passions
Day after day. Every line
Bears witness to what?
Fragments of light?
Light striking towers.

Nothing came before the word.
More and more the days
Are erected beyond memory,
Beyond silence, beyond
Proportions. They uncouple from hope
As fire does from the word.

We have always been in heaven.
High above the landscape,
Staring through the windows
In wonder before our own breath.

CHINESE SUITS

We were invited to the trial
But somehow the children got confused
Or were unable to handle any information
That came from the world outside
Their heads. We were sorry for them.

The entire field became transparent.
There were guardians dressed in Chinese
Suits and carrying huge swords.
They probably wouldn't have hurt
Anyone, but there was no way to be sure.

Headlights flooded the sides of the road
Near the bridge. Even this far back
We could hear the tires squealing and
See the blue smoke. The sound of metal
Crunching sounded like someone eating.

Reflections began popping back and forth
From the shields carried by the servants.
They had their own concerns and we were
Just as dreamers to them. Whatever
We did, whatever we decided, would
Seem as nothing to them. They gave
Us jobs to keep us busy. The children
Sat and watched us as if they could learn something.

CROSSING THE RIVER

And still he smiled.
The clouds hung
Themselves, becoming
Red then violet
The blood drifting
Through them stretching
The sky inside them.

And still he smiled.
The fish swam into
The hollows
Of his head and waited
Unblinking, the water
Rushing past above them.

And still he smiled.
A huge bear grew in his mind
And began tearing at the brain
His eyes clouding over, skull
Bursting, the dark fish
Caught in the heavy hand of the bear.

GENESIS

There used to be a house right here
Where I am standing. Now there is just
Your body and my hands are a surgeon's.
I lift your organs and remove the part that breaks
Whenever you see me standing in the rain.

What language did we speak then?
What were those words you said?
I cannot recall them now. It seems
They were put together places,
Smelling of bleak hotel rooms,
Small tears in the imagination
Impossible to put together once
The runs began to race toward
Your thighs, spreading the fabric
Greater and greater distances,
Until I can once more see the moon
High above whatever city we were in.

The lions still move at the bottom of the stairs,
Snakes winding about the columns.
They know we are here. They don't have
To look for us. They know the picture
Is theirs and they will ask us "What do you
Want more than anything?"

To fall asleep, not knowing my name.
Not knowing your name. Not
Having any name at all and to be touching
Your body with all that I am, hearing the first
Word. It is coming from your mouth.

GIOTTO'S ANGELS

Their lamentations are endless.
Their garments laced with painful
Lines as they tear their clothing,
Pull their hair from their heads.
Today one can stand among them,
Draped with gold leaf and transformed.
We can be these angels. They infect
Our eyes with their twisted splendor.
We know exactly what they have seen.

Where I am today, they hover over the river.
They have become herons and egrets.
No less angels, they remain the passion
Beneath the beauty of every moment.
The gardens have sprung from the sloughs,
Sprung from the body of a dead Christ.
This can speak even here, centuries later.
We remain in the realm of angels.
We live in the next world. We lick Giotto's
History with our tongues. The dead Christ,
Now a landscape, envelopes us completely.

We are able still to lean over the body
Of the delta and see those angels
Above us, every movement grief and anguish
Exploding in the dark sky. Each part touched
By a perfection of gold leaf and unfailing belief
In angels, always angels, always their lamentations.

THE KING OF BIRDS

The celestial forest.
A pine wind.
Storms in the mountains.

The stars have little place to sleep.
Always unraveling, a dumb mouth
Sits in the center of all birds.

The mute swan flapping its wings
Furiously. I know your name.
I know the king of birds.

I have to ask you this
Before it gets too late
And you can't find a way
Out of this poem.
Did you guess this was going
To happen? That you might
Find yourself crying over nothing?
That you truly have been abandoned
In the forest and that the king of birds
Was going to turn out to be a lie
You told just so someone would
Marry you?

Even if you knew the names of your children
And could see the sacred heart hanging
Across a street, bold as a lie, blood dripping
From the crown of thorns as you fell to your knees?

I am afraid I understand all of this too well.
That you will take my hand, or I will take
Your hand and we will set out to find an altar,
But will wind up going to dinner and will have
Too much wine and the tablecloth will catch
On fire. We will see the flocks of birds, so many
Different kinds, flee before us and you will ask

If I would like dessert and I will want you naked
And go stumbling across the floor, trying to dance.
We have guests in the house and you had asked
Me to tell the story of how I met the king of birds
But no one is listening. I can't forget that time.

You light a cigarette. I can see you standing
On the island just across the harbor. You are
Wearing that yellow dress. I am standing
On the edge of the pier, still talking, while they
Are untying the boat, starting the motor.
But I still am not done talking and the transmission
Is breaking up and who gives a shit anyway.
The night is so beautiful and not too cool.
The moon is on the lake. We are going out
Now, before it is too late, to see the king of birds.

PENULTIMATE

I've got this house in the desert.
They won't find us there.
You can wear a rose in your hair.
Tomorrow is close, still small, still inert.

You showed me the knife blade.
It almost glowed when I touched it.
Who was going to believe we were here?
We shredded our clothing as it got darker.

We stood on either side of the window
So we could see the streets. A patrol
Was walking slowly up the avenue
With their dogs and their rifles
Cradled in their arms like something dead.

The streetlight across the way would flicker
Then go out for a few minutes.
That was our signal to leave.
I grabbed your forearm and pulled
You near to me. 'Listen, this is all
We have left. We will meet on the other
Side of the river. Stay close to the buildings.'

When I saw the video later, I couldn't help
But notice that you were biting your lips hard.
I put my hands on the screens. I could feel you
In the flickering light. Things would be okay.
The children told me you would be here in the morning.
I kissed the back of my hands. They were trembling so.

SPEAKING IN EXPLETIVES

I can drive cars into my imagination.
They have no brakes. They have
Lots of lights.

A separate rain. The burns across
The palms of my hands. I read
With my eyes closed. The night
Air fills with huge sparks.
I choose to live like this.

I can hear stars chanting.
"Shut up. People will think
You've caused something."
A morning filled with old clocks.

An algebra of regrets filled with eagles.
All of this dust was once armies.
All of poetry, a concordance of possibilities.
Shadows of invisible monuments.
Decisions made by flowing water.

Fish begging for a greater understanding
Of fireflies and the history of night.
The radiant trappings draped upon the heart.
What echo says to each precious moment.

You'll have a better idea of this
When everything is perfect.
Help me lift these words in tribute
To eternity. Eternity will remember you
For this. It will kiss you on the lips.

The tides mimic our emotions.
Long ago I walked with lions.
Just get into the boat quickly.
We will not want to miss the sunrise.

TALKING TO THE STARS

I was selling fireworks to the stars.
They have no home. They were happy
To see me. They asked about piano music.
They said it had been so long since they
Heard any of it and that last night the moon
Was so silvery and golden that they remembered
How beautiful it could be. I noticed that the stars
All wore rings on their fingers. They told me
It was because they were married to so many memories
And carried them in their flaming hearts.

They told me that the Night had problems
Of its own but never grumbled. That wasn't
Its job. They laughed when I said it kept
Things hidden. "Just like crows." they said.

Most of the stars live in trailers.
It makes it easy to go from place to place.
I've seen them in lover's eyes and whirling
Around the head of cartoon characters
And tugging on the fishing lines of
Winkin', Blinken', and Nod. Poetry
Is loaded with them. They love the attention.

FAULT LINES

Sometimes the fault line, sometimes the fault.
There will be consequences for all the actions
Taken here, the wind, the rain, the mornings without
Incident when we neglected to differentiate between
One day and another, believing each day was just
Like another because our surroundings remained
the same. One cannot trust to consciousness

To explain change. People die totally unnoticed.
The kind of music they loved may appear in a dream
Shifting between call and response, Ol' Hannah,
Then that sound of hammer against huge steel nails.

We struggle and swim ashore. "Are you having
A good time?' The ground beneath our feet
Opens and the tectonic plates move slightly,
Not much, just enough to bring down Los Angeles.

Our feelings are electric. They belong to the realm
Bounded by animals, guarded by animals, surrounded
By others who bear a resemblance to ourselves but
Will always remain other. We still choose to call them
Brother, afraid that if we do not we will no longer be able
To read the book, stand in lines with them waiting to get in.

This is a form of praying or so I am told by the swirl
Time puts on on our presence here. There will be
Consequences for all the actions taken.
Sometimes the fault line, sometimes the fault.

TOWARD LOVE

And somehow you can't be afraid
Of anything. If you are going
To open your mouth to talk about
Love, there can be no part of it,
Or of your body, that doesn't remove
All of its garments and reach out naked
Toward embrace or get hit with the back
Of a hand, or met with words that once
Had meaning other than what one might
Have ever imagined. And what is your safe word?
It can't have anything to do with what might
Be done to that body or what your body
Might be doing to the body of someone else.

There is a terror as the foot slips
From the edge of the curb, the sidewalk
Wet, the grass too slick, and you pitch
Forward or backward and it feels good
Or it doesn't feel good and your mouth
Begins to bleed no matter how it feels.

Your fingernails dig into the back of your lover
And the marks look like words.
And the words sound like dogs barking.
You can feel your head pitch
Back and slam into the sidewalk.
Concussion. Maybe. The entire idea
Of love may even see you living your
Life unable to walk correctly again.

But you can't stop the love.
So you speak of the weather
Or something you felt just before
Your head smashed into the concrete,
Just before the blood broke through
Your skin and you forget what it was
You were saying. All you can taste

Is that taste that might be blood,
Or might be wet grass. Your ears
Filled with so many sounds you must
Struggle just to hear the words,
Just to know what you want the words
To mean.

You are actually saying them to someone
And more than you might want religion
Or sex or someone making you feel
Like you just learned how to invent
Your body, you realize that all there is
Are these words you've managed to hold.

They are like a streetlight,
Like a morning, like a mouth
Moving on your body,
Like your darkest fantasy has just
Been able to afford its own car
And it stops and sees you
Wet and sprawled on the edge
Of the street. And it opens the door
Of the car and looks at you lying there,
So full of desire, all of your being
Struggling to hold these words
Close in your bloody mouth,
Your damaged head.

And it says, "Get in the car now!
You know what you want!
Get in the fucking car now!

THE COSMIC ASYLUM
for Skar Plow

Something broke behind my eyes.
I was able to see great flights of birds
In a fictive space within my skull.

The day threatened rain but never
Pulled the trigger. I could taste the water
On my lips, almost swim in it, but I knew
It did not remember me at all.

When I looked down I could see
A river, with a mouth like Neruda making love.
And the sun was an evening mist that made
Color dance. I wanted my skin to be like that.

Darkness promises me particular things
But I refuse them. It begins to pursue me
With blood stains and rivers of which
I cannot see the banks. I can feel my destiny
Touch me in my most intimate places, laughing
As if it has discovered something about me
Which I cannot know without living thousands
Of days more, listening for the horsemen,
Rushing to the shadows when I hear the hooves
Thunder closer and closer. From here I can see
The circle about to close. I write furiously, attending
To the preciousness of words as if they were my children.

THE SMALLEST ROOM

One wall was of eyes.
One wall was of thunder.
One wall was of lies.

One wall was of wonder.
One window looked upon the sea.
One window saw the sun rise.
One window looked beyond the trees.

One window looked back inside.
One wall held painting.
One wall held a clock.
One wall had a doorway
But the door was always locked.

THE BAY

The lights were going on and off.
I could see your mouth moving.
The lights made your teeth look
Like cars sliding onto an exit ramp.

There was no sound. So I may tell you
Whatever seemed perfect for that moment.
Don't drain the batteries just to keep
The lights going. Everyone knows they go.

There was a backdrop of images, all of Krishna
Except for tondos of tigers wrestling
That were left over from when the music
We made had electronic references.

It was okay to say I love you
Once again. The lighting was understated.
It was much too beautiful
To think you'd be walking away.

THE OUTSKIRTS OF THE CITY

There is never a direction here.
I can wrap the entire place
In silk that forms a secret body
Of streets and secret meetings
Which live only in our blood
Passing through the heart.

Naming names and mornings,
Victories and defeats,
Empty palaces, torches
Still burning. Corridors
Damp with leaving and heartbreak.
Fear and more corridors of sleep.

Our flesh has messages for us.
We mostly choose to ignore
Their admonitions. There is
No place, no useful memory,
No poem that grants us absolution
Without demanding everything we remember.

Promising to hold it until everything else
We ever knew has been forgotten.

THE OTHER RELIGION
For Robert L. Wagner

Forty four coats of Coronado Red,
Rubbing each coat out in-between.
Smoother than lipstick and butter
To look at, gleam in the night when
The garage door is popped open.

The air is a cloud of lacquer spray.
There must be no wind. Nothing
But air gonna touch this car. My,
My, my, how it shine. Only thing
Better is a Fender guitar lying in
Its case. Only thing sweeter is
Everyone just standing around
Waiting on Summer midnight,
Smoking cigarettes and looking
Deep into the paint, seeing their
Lives in there, reflecting back.

So many of them could never get
Over how it was being there,
How it felt, how everything looked.
So that stayed. For more than thirty
Years they continued to talk, to smoke,
To paint the cars, work on them, transform
Them so that they matched a single moment.

THE PARTING

We will wait for the moon tonight.
It is not only the moon. It is full
And we can see it through the rain.

It is not like you are a child.
I will put the moon in my mouth
And we can stay in bed. I will
Pass it into your mouth when we kiss.

I will tell you a story of a warrior I knew.
He used a rabbit skin to make a beard.
We lost him in the famous snows
That winter. When we found his body
In the Spring he was in full armor
And looked more fearful than a trap
Set to catch a tiger that terrible Winter.

I am going to continue North.
Meet me under the trees
And you can use my heart
As a pillow all the while I am gone.

THE MERCHANTS
for Maqroll 'el Gaviero'

I can no longer determine which childhood was mine.
I can see the precarious structure upon which dreams
Are made. I can see how truths bear
The mark of the incommunicable.

I was watching you stroll along the pier,
Glancing into the water, lifting your eyes
To the horizon. Here, in the North the days
Are either too short or much too long.

I squeeze the colors between my fingers.
I will paint the midnight and it will be full
Of horses, gifts of the moon, a brightness
I will not be able to hold in my arms
As I once held you. I too watch the surf,
How it seems to have a language,
How the waves tease at its back,
Making the conversation impossible to stop.

Someone has come to me in the night
To sell me memories. They are cheap.
They can become your own by reading things
Like this. "What are you feeling?" they ask.

I swear this happened to you when you were
Only four years old. Why, your mother herself told me
It was so. That screaming has been torn from
A throat no longer able to speak. You can hear
Them wash upon the shingled beach, a thousand
Voices. Any of them could be yours.

Tonight, I will stand near the bow and watch
You walk along, above the water, thinking
Whatever it is you may be thinking.

I have a photograph of you doing exactly this.
It was taken years ago. See, you look so young.
Do not fear any encounter. Look, the birds turn
And wheel above your head. They too are memories.
How many do you need? How foolish I am to ask.

ONE NIGHT STAND

Come with me now to the thrilling days of yesteryear.
The streets of Aberdeen are full of water.
The Wolf Moon eating the hills all through the night.
I see you when I look to the North. I remember
The lavender you sent me when you wore lamb's wool
And leopard fur. I could feel the sting of the weather
Even then. I said, "What do you think of this?"

A thick sunset crackling like a fishing boat
Full of the silver of fish bodies. Use your own
Body to do to me again what the light does to my lips
Tonight. Harvesting words out of the East
That cause illustrious dreaming on a night such as this.

The flood waters spread out so wide. Do not use
Your thoughts. Do you know how much I love you?
You are my misfortune, an inexhaustible flesh that reaches
The limit of what I can understand, fragments of angels
Not made of time as we are, instant after instant,

I disappear into the small hands of the rain that I had
Heard tell of. Darkness closes in. It wears goodbye
Like a cloudy mirror, constantly jumping off myths
Of ourselves, stories we have become even as we
Become the fish in the boats, the hollow of the Wolf Moon,
The torn wings off fairies barely able to contain light.

Come with me now. We will shake the mountain.
We will climb one into another again and again,
So what is the good in talking about it any longer?
Mirrors pulling the sky over us helping us to a season of infinity,
Or, if we are really lucky, toward something we can call morning.

OUR WHOLE LIFE

"Our woal life is a idear we dint think of
nor we don't know what it is. What a way to live."
Riddley Walker

The eye lights blinked out.
The fire still reflected on them.

Larrin had caught a spear in him
Just before we got there and was
Mostly gone when we came to his place.

He saw them in the black wood and
He threw a rock at them to scare
Them, but they didn't scare.
They stopped and one of them threw
The spear. It went right through
Him and he was mostly dead before
He hit the ground, except for his eyes.

Just outside the door
Two men were whispering together.
"This wouldn't have happened
If there was a wing.
This was a disappearing and nothing
Alive could twist the blood
And put it back into a man."

"Something out there is feeding on us,
Making a soup of the homeless
And the whores and the bones
Of the poor."

We began to listen to the stars.
They were like beating hearts.
It was somehow wondrous as
Our heads began to talk and we spoke
Of fiery kingdoms and things of
Wonder we could not comprehend.
The sky moved so slowly above us

It seemed that it had forgotten
Something, something gentle that
Could no longer be gentle,
That made the hands bleed
When touched by our perfection.

We watched the wind form
Around us, pushing us as the night
Does a branch.

The spear had been cleaned
And was intent on resuming its life
As a tree. Oh where shall
We go now? Where shall we go?

We sat down at the table.
We too were clean.
We too had a place in the mystery.

The woods bristled with the shells,
Thick as ignorance, cracking
As we huddled near that door.

We could smell the sea.
The ancient islands. We could
See the luminous heads
Begin to rise above the trees.
We cannot stay here any longer.
Leave his body with the children.
They will lift it with their white
And pale little hands.

Give it to the rain.
Give it to whatever holds the world
Together.
It is quiet here for a moment.
There is no longer any room for us.
Oh love, turn your star on,
Just for a moment.
The secret will be in its radiance.

NOVEMBER

The late afternoon sun
Coming in low across the birch
Trees and the liquid ambers
Making their yellows and reds,
An adagio of sorts, As if it burned
What little warmth left in the day
Into our eyes allowing us to wonder
At the quick change toward early
Dark to hazed fog balanced in its night,

Had found itself locked in the high
Bedroom two floors above the bread
Smell kitchen, unable to leave the room.

Perhaps the room thought it was an ornament
That belonged to it alone or that
It was a dance, some unknown overture
That needed to be confined within
The room with its bed and dresser,
Its white linen curtains and bed
Clothing, but it held on
Well into the late hours when I,
Going to bed, noticed it trying to
Escape through the smallest of spaces
Between the door and the floor.

I entered the room and in the quick
Moments before it fled, I saw
The dread it carried for the coming
Months of Winter, even as it spread
Itself across the furniture and begged
The light to release it. Reflections
In the small mirror, cutting the edge
Of the photograph of the young couple
Taken during the Second World War,
Clipping the curve of the pillows.
Roving up the edge of the partially

Opened closet, furious to leave
The room and end the day.

It flowed around and over me,
Flashing against the bannister,
Catching the mullions of the windows,
Spilling the night back into the room,
Making ghosts of all within, its
Glow firing itself in my memory
That such a thing were even possible.

I stood for a long moment watching
The change flood the room.
From what was truly impossible
But had actually happened before
My eyes.

This was a gift not freely
Given by any day and I began
To recognize that childhood had
Returned with a moment's magic
Before I was once again old
In what I knew and believed
To be true.

NOT SLEEPING

Where is the poem?
Too tired to put its little
Feet on the rungs of the ladder
In order to reach the place where
It can finally see over the top
Of the wall in a quiet neighborhood

Where the twilight shows tiny points
Of light, lamps being lit in windows
So soft that melodies come from
Them like sighs or glances taken
In leaving some loved place
For the last time.

The million mistakes we make
Trying to find where it can go next
And then seeing it sleeping next
To us in bed, late in the evening
Breathing the breath of the lover.

SKY WITHOUT A NAME

...a vision

Say this then, that I have known
You better than waves know the shingle
On the shore of the sea that speaks to
It, at telling of its presence, its golden
Robes, shadows deeper than the memory
China dresses up and presents as a tiger.

Crossing the sky without a name,
Claiming that it is beautiful, while a bird,
A most beautiful bird, a white one
With the head of a wolf pounces
Upon us full of those damned flowers
That keep us from all committing suicide
In the light of such a setting sun
Too incredible to be believed.

Pleasure in a warm young bird.
The sky drifting high above us,
Feeling this on our skin like leaves
That fall on our graves with every hour we linger,
With every star we dare to name.

MERCY

She, at the end of mercy
Had heard a song
And it came to have
A meaning.

A vacant loss surrounded
By a silence that could
Not move closer to my lips.

It would not have words.
Rather, it would be a membrane
That keeps the guts
In their place while
We walk the planet,
Then touches us, insisting
That we must answer some
Kind of call.

Tonight, the rain continues
Softly, opening the earth.
This disappears the words
Syllable by syllable,
Vowel by vowel.
Consonant by consonant,
Until, standing, near
Midnight at my open door
I can hear the coyotes
Explaining such mercy
To their hungry cubs.

CROW VISION

And the crows flew.
There were ten or twelve,
But one came back toward me
And I became afraid.

But it circled me slowly
And made me still.
Then, landing on my shoulder
While I quivered in fear
Spoke in a crow voice
Saying:

We saw your face below the ice,
Looking at us as we gathered
For the night. And then you
Walked across the frozen
Field and we saw you
As star light, but closer
And knew you could hear
Us talking of masks
And flaming ropes
And the precise qualities
Of the wind this drear
Evening and wondered why
You chose to come to us now?

Are you a portent?
What have you seen?

I have known you all my life,
I said and have found
It unbearable that you crows
Still feel I am less a bird,
Perhaps a madness, to you.
For I am trees and weather
And feathers and spine.

But now I am not
Alarmed, no not at all.
I do gaze up at you
From below the ice
And now unfold as leaves
To you and your clan.

And in the morning
I will be gone again.
Lying in my bed, waking
Gazing across the winter gardens,
Listening to you talk. But I
Shall no longer know the
Language of the crows.

Yes, this is so, he said and lifted
His wings and became
The night once more.

FIREFLIES

I meant to say something
Completely different
But I kept thinking of your eyes
And what your neck must
Feel like if I found the right
Place to place my lips upon
it, so you could recognize
What I was doing was kissing you.

I could have thought of the puritanical sky
But you would not have
Recognized any sky.

I had to imagine our tongues
Intertwining and fields and streams
Coming to tell you that
I was loving you.

That all these words
Were not fireflies.

TEARS AND THEIR CHILDREN

The room had no ceiling.
Someone had recently taken
The stars out for their evening walk
And they remained excited by the
Moon.

Tears were suspended in the air.
We could walk between some of
Them and hear their voices full
To the brim with the joy and sorrows
They contained.

I cannot name the beasts who dwelt
There. They had faces like people
We all knew. So few of them had
Names.

They were the vermin of politics,
Blind to most all of who walked
These beautiful plains.

I have been asked not to speak
Of the rivers of blood but to dwell
Upon the bliss possible at the edge
Night collects about itself before
All turns to darkness.

I should mention a kiss
And not speak of the mangled,
Distraught and mad who walk beside
Us everyday. Why would you care
About such things when the stars
Are as eager as puppies to please
Your imagination.

I have been told I must end this way
Of talking and leave such journeys
To those unable to dream.
Look, even now they come to stop…

THE GREATEST OF MUSEUMS

The house was only that big
Because of his collection.
Acres and acres of protected
Spaces.

He collected ship wrecks.
Not models or photographs
But entire ships, even
The rocks they had
Crashed upon. Tableaux.

A huge field tied
To the little flea
Of human history.

Tiny blots of light
Somewhere in the midst
Of the sea. Lamp
Swinging in the captain's quarters.

The ocean opens its mouth
To speak.
The greatest of museums.
Famous ships that had
Been used by time
To have stories for
Those starved by the world.

In the final room
A wall of dim light
Circled the room.

"Here is where it happened."
Lights and the sound
Of waves crashing
Against the shoreline.

Just as it does now,
As you are reading this.

THE TOY TRAIN

She said it was a toy train.
It was made of spider webs.
It disappeared through a closed door
Not like any train I had ever seen before.

My dog came through the mirror
Without a sound, without a sidelong glance. .
Derelict, abandoned, a room without a floor.
The train could move inside a dream facade.
Littered with old memories, their meaning gone
Like rain that through a broken window pane might pour.

And I dwelt there through a thousand nights
Caught by the grey of shadows, a prisoner
Of the moon, a captive of the spirits that
Dwell inside my bones, a distant ringing
Of a bell across the quickening season.
Masked, unmasked, another mask and then no more

WHERE THE STARS
ARE KEPT

1. A HANDFUL OF STARS

THE MILKY WAY

We live in a spiral arm of a spinning
Field of stars, we whirl around, a carnival
Ride, full of birds, loves, emotions, endless
Varieties of things unfolding in seasons;
Full of bells and an endless weaving of hearts.

These connections ride upon our consciousness,
Demanding constant performance from us.
Each of us, most royal and majestic as night,
Vile, vindictive and spoiled even before we speak;
Sorrow and joy, the way we sound our name.

We endure all of this, our lips kissing each moment,
Crushed, elated, misunderstood, praised for things
We do as part of ourselves, damned for these same things.

There is no road, there is no plan. Only love
Survives.

Everything is forgiven, finally.
Understanding limps behind the parade,
Always late, always burdened with qualifications,
Always abandoning every opinion and argument,
Leaving each of us our place only, describing
This place, the swirling arms, the myriad ways
We twist ourselves to achieve
This weaving, this carnival of love.

BIRTHPLACE: NIAGARA FALLS, NY

When I reached the middle of the Rainbow
Bridge they had just turned on the colored
Lights. Vibrant arms reached across the gorge,
Trapping fields of mist, shattering individual
Droplets, bathing everything in primary colors,
Tints and shades of blue and green, pinks
Pulling on the edges of the Bridal Veil Falls.

I was overwhelmed by the sight. I had seen
It hundreds, maybe a thousand times before;
Every time was as the first. Such light,
Such water, such distance, such a place.
There was never a dream like this. Living
Here made this vision "normal," every night,
The lights, white, then color, then white,
Then nothing. The pale water still falling.
The endless sound permeating all of space.

I stood still for over an hour, just looking.
This was mine. This place, my birthplace.
There would be no way to tell others what
It was like. They would never understand.

I decided I had to leave these things to create
Something else full of these things, but in
A different form. I had a small idea of what
It would be like, how it would sound,
How it could be made to feel. I produced books,
Magazines, broadsides. Copy after copy
Flying off the press, full of important and
Essential information. When I close my eyes
At night, those lights still smash against the
Falling water. The roar of the Falls sounding
Like words far in the distance. I sleep this way.

WHERE THE STARS ARE KEPT
(for Tom Kryss)

In a small drawer about eight
Inches wide, two and one half
Inches high and about a foot deep.

The drawer is in a plain-looking
Chest of drawers in a back room.
It has a keyhole and can be locked.
It seldom is, however, as it is opened
With great regularity by anyone
Needing stars. Although the drawer
Is unmarked, it is not hidden in any
Way. Those who need stars can
Obtain them at any time.

Once I pulled the drawer almost
All the way out and just looked
Into it for a long time. The
Stars twinkled and glittered. They seemed
To float in the blackness of the drawer.
It was very quiet in the room. I
Reached into the drawer and touched
Some stars. They were cool then hot,
Slippery feeling. I could hold many
Stars in my hand at one time without
Any effort. This was a long time ago.

2. TWO LIES

THE PLACE WHERE WE ALWAYS HEARD CRYING

When we walked to Crozier's little store to buy candy and other stuff, there was a lot (we called it a field) that was about half of a block long and a block wide. There was a beaten path through it because the street that went to the store stopped at the lot on the far side and the path was the easiest way to get there.
In this lot one could always be sure that, while walking across it, one would hear
someone crying. Not always the same person or the same volume but always crying or sobbing that came from somewhere, maybe in the neighborhood, we never knew.
We didn't think it was unusual at the time. We would say to each other, "There it is," or "Listen, I'll bet you somebody is crying again." It was just after World War II, so it was probably a real thing. We never found out and there are houses on the spot now.

THE BLACK LINE

Where the trees ended at what is now the edge of a city park,
there was, at one time, a long black line about two inches wide
that stretched almost a quarter of a mile perfectly straight. It
was perfectly even on its edges its entire length. Nothing grew
on it for about eight years. Kerry said that one time when he
stood on it for awhile he could hear people talking, but they
seemed far away.
Once I walked its length, stepping on it the entire way. I could
hear singing in a foreign language and recall that pictures of a
village where violet flowers grew stayed in my head until I
stepped off the line.
Nothing grew there.
Dogs didn't like it at all and barked whenever we crossed it.
One time my brother Bob stood on one end of the line and I
stood on the other. We thought we could talk to each other
very clearly without even using words.
We were probably imagining things.
When they made the park and plowed that part of the woods,
the machines they used broke down every day for a week.
There is nothing there now at all.

BURNING GREEN WOOD

Once in Spring, I saw a heart
Smoldering atop a fire of green
Wood. "Pruning fire," the farmer told
Me when I came closer to watch.
"Looks like a heart in there," I said,
Pointing. "Reckon so," he answered. "Came
Out of the pears." He gestured to the
Orchard. "Kind of unusual, no?" I offered.
"Found 'em before," he said, poking at it
With a long-handled rake. "After Winter
There's lots of stuff comes out of pruning. I've found
Boxes of letters. Lots of dreams, well, parts
Of them anyway. They don't last long usually.
Even found prayers, once or twice. Think
People would take better care with them."
The heart caught fire, flamed briefly then
Quieted down again. "Out here's a good
Place to leave things," he continued,
"Puppies, kittens, a body once,
Nobody knew who it was.
Things that are hard to lose, have to put
Them someplace. Think that heart's been
There all Winter. Looked pretty battered."
"Kind of sad, isn't it?" I asked.
"Always is," he said, looking me in the face.
"Better than after the war though. There were
A lot of them then. That's why I use
Green wood, new growth. Makes lots
Of smoke, yes, but it's new stuff.
Seems better to do it like this." He shifted
His weight and threw more wood
On the flames, covering the heart altogether.
"What are you doing out here?" he asked.
"Walking, I like long walks."
"Good thing, walks," he said. "Have a nice one."
"Thank you," I replied and started away,
The smell of wood smoke in my nostrils,
The tower of it reaching high above

The orchard. The sky still morning pink.
A sound of songbirds came, first far away,
Then closer, insisting that the moment
Indeed be Spring, all else of no matter whatsoever.

PAPERS DYED BLUE

There was a room
Beneath the stairs,
Not for brooms, too small,
Yet large enough for two
With a bit more space to spare.

I had discovered it
While very young.
No one else knew.
The house was old.
Some other child had brought
Their treasure there, a special
Ring, a mirror, a kind of map,
A bear, all untouched
One hundred years or more,
Waiting for me to find them.

I brought things too.
Some books, my Star Wars
Toys, one hundred papers I had
Dyed in different shades of blue.

We moved when I was eleven.
No one else knew. I left
My things there too; an offering.
Someone else would find this
Place too. I do not know who
Lives there now. I am far away.
If you see this and remember
Such a place, perhaps it's you.

A NEW LIE

For a time while I was growing up, I went to the movies on
Saturday afternoons.
Prices were low; there were usually short subject, serials,
news and other features beside the main event. Walking
from our house in Kenmore to either of two theaters was al-
ways an adventure. They were further than we were usually
allowed to roam and it made us, my brother and our friends,
feel more grown up.
The Granada Theater was the farthest away and we were not
as familiar with the streets in that part of town, around the
University of Buffalo, as we were other areas. In the Fall, the
early onset of evening made the trek even more exciting.
One evening after seeing a film at the Granada, our little
crowd was returning home when we were confronted by a
group of older boys we didn't know. They were aggressive
and called us names. They began to chase us. We were very
afraid and hoped we could cross Sheridan Drive into our
own neighborhood before they caught us. We felt that they
meant to beat us up for some reason. We ran hard. As we
passed under the streetlights on the tree-lined avenues, the
dark seemed to be everywhere around us. Occasionally, we
would turn and look back at our pursuers, calculating the
distance between us and them. After a couple of blocks, one
of us noticed that when these demons passed underneath a
streetlight, they seemed to become suddenly brighter and
almost transparent. We told each other about this and made
efforts to notice what was happening as we ran. They
seemed to become very bright, almost a grapefruit color, for
a second or two and then faded back to dark, becoming
voices only.
I forget who it was that said that this was extremely weird,
but we agreed. After the next streetlight we ducked into a
clump of bushes at the corner of a street, hiding. The boys
came through the streetlight and indeed they did glow.
They seemed to have little substance. It was like we could
see through them. They ran past our hiding place. They
glowed for awhile, transparent, and then their voices faded
and they seemed to evaporate into the night time.

We waited a long while before giving up our hiding place and running back to the neighborhood just as fast as if they were chasing us.

We talked about the pursuit as we regained our breath, but no one ever mentioned how this event ended. I think we were incapable of believing it had happened. Perhaps we generated this event through our own fears of being in an unfamiliar neighborhood at dusk. Whatever occurred that evening remains quite remarkable in memory.

THEY HAD GIVEN ME A HANDFUL OF STARS

And told me I could go down to the lake
When the evening grew long and toss them
Out across the water to watch
The colors they would make.

It grew quite loud in the dream.
I couldn't drive the beasts back
With my voice. Sound had abandoned
All things and the ropes of joy
Lashed out at me. No one would
Ever get home from this one.
I looked at their eyes.

When I saw you walking along the shoreline
I was already too tired to hear anymore.
You looked as if someone had managed
To fill you up with children playing alone
On rainy afternoons. The wind moved your
Dress like a thousand flags
Excited by the parade of you.
I began to throw the stars out
Across the water.

She was next to me watching them skip
And sputter and finally shine deep within
The lake, wavering. "All these stars," she
Said, "What for?" And the dogs began snapping
At my ankles and I wanted to throw them all
In her face and scream at her. "You
Don't need stars in here at all," she said.

And I continued to toss them one by one
Until the whole night was lit up bright
As any room, all the while looking into
Her eyes at the reflections. Silver lances
Stuck into the sand, we remained motionless
Like this, somehow outside time and still
Creatures of it.

DELIVERING THE MAIL

A long low sound, as if a train
Somewhere in the night began
To address an imagined audience
With whistles and rhythmic pulses.
From here it sounds like a voice
Gathering itself and then dispersing again.

There are messages on the back
Of the night; certainly translations
That never quite realize themselves.

They catch on dreams, cluster
Like wind-driven leaves.
Oftentimes we wake to hear
An instant of the insistence.

All that creates sound moves
This energy again and again,
Refining, gathering, coalescing.
Occasionally we are sure
We recognize it. We abide its
Sweet flow as we rise from sleep.
By nightfall it has completely
Disappeared. The wind, the wind, directs
The sound of leaves over the night,
Passing in long breaths, simulating
Language. We imagine we understand
These sounds.

Pretend then, in words.
I write you a letter about this.
You reply that it is amazing
Mail reaches us at all;
That it contains such significance
As it moves past our eyes;
That it tries to explain, tells of a yearning

Or that we love each other as we do.
It becomes remarkable.
It sounds far away
As those trains
Noticed just before we come to understand
That this is not music we are hearing.

WHAT WE HEAR
For Leslie

Just before you go to sleep
A quick movement arrests
Your attention. It is seemingly
Close, a gesture perhaps, emphatically
Demanding your attention now.
The soft light of dreaming lifts
Your hand in greeting. Something
Like a song begins to form
In your mouth. A melody
Draped with afternoons in late Spring,
The way she looked at you on
A certain day. The highway
Unfurling before you, always more
Roads. You can hear the chords.
The changes. You wave back intimately.
It seems like it has been years
Since you've seen it. You fall in love.

RAINING

It is raining and I am memory,
I am listening to the moments,
Wearing boots and walking just
To hear the sound of splashes
As it wounds the puddles
With the ashes of warm rooms.

It is raining and I am memory,
Sheets of rooster tails turned
Up by automobiles as they tear
The evening apart with headlights,
The hissing of tires in the rain.

It is raining and I am memory
And you are there beyond all this,
Diamonds on your eyelashes,
Sparkles on your lips, a welter
Of words whispered into my ears.

It is raining and I am memory
Washing the edges of the street in sheets
Of weather, smashing into your
Face, naked as water is naked,
All sound and wind fury,
All language reduced to splatters
On the window glass, all rain all memory
Washing like a heart upon the past.

LUNA ISLAND

On this street most of the lights are broken.
As we stroll from pool to pool of light the night
Has dances for us and moves the wind across our clothes,
Tosses our hair, throws some rain and touches us
Quietly, as if we could understand what it says.

I am broken this cold evening. I can
Understand little, grab your hand and put
It inside the jacket pocket with mine for a while.
Let the fingers talk to each other, Words have gone.

I would like to tell you about how beautiful
The lights are at Niagara Falls, when they
Illuminate the water at night, but you would
Not understand. The low and constant moaning
Of the water, day and night for over 12,000 years
Now is its own kind of music, locked in Dolomite
And the collapse of shale from irregular cliffs.

I can hear the sound of our footsteps in the
Pools of the dark. Small rainbows circle the streetlights
As we near them. I wish that they had voices,

It has been so long since we spoke to each other
Like this, where words were everything and everything
Was truth and your fingers against mine were small
Songs that used our hearts to keep the time.

"You got here too late," I tell you.
Now I am blessed with longing only and you
Are blessed with a desire to know the dawn
As it has never been known before.

You laugh and tell me not to worry. "Listen,"
I say. "Can you hear time making sweeps up
And down the deep gorge, hovering just above the rap-
ids?"

"No, I can hear only singing, it's like someone
Was trying to tell me something important. Can you
Hear it too?" I answer "yes" but that it is spoken
In a different language. "Say something in that language,"
You say. "Okay, I squeeze your hand and kiss you."

"It's like that," I say. "I understand," you say.
"I really do." I believe you until we reach the
Next streetlight and the conversation changes.

LOOKING AT THE WAY THE NIGHT SITS DOWN

It has a way of talking that has
Nothing to do with words.

Like, in dreams, when you
Find yourself forced
Awake because of something that
Happened, in a dream,
A kiss, yes or more a motion
The way a hand moved
Or a particular sound that
Reminds one of a feeling.

In a dream, yes there,
No place else, no reality to make a stain
Upon your life and then again
Perhaps that is the flower.

We open our eyes.
We are outside, naked
Against the night.
In a dream
The stars are hissing their stories at us.
We are able to understand them
If only for a moment.

What we hear is love,
Nothing small about it
Total, unrequited, but real.

We wait for morning
Touching our bodies,
Thinking that this sensation
May be all that there is,
All that there is — bird songs

Drums folding the night into
Rhythm
Breathing hard
Against all we understand
Only to understand even more.

I reach into the sky, easy.
I feel your fingertips.
They are touching mine.
I don't believe it.

THIS KIND OF MUSIC

We have found a dance.
It was unexpected, nestled
Under a bush, near the edge
Of the lake, a song that
Fish would love.

Air rising and falling.
Listen: I am moving my mouth
Upon your mouth and we are
Looking for words. The evening
Has gloves and eases us into
A small room where everything
That is the world is not allowed.

You touch me like all that is summer,
Like the easing of the heart as it
Comes to recognize what is true
In music and in speaking.

I speak to you. You become
A dance I have never understood
Until this moment. I stand up.
I dance with you. Listen
To this kind of music.

HOW IS THE HEART EMBRACED

How does it change its name? Caught
In pools of blood, its pulse
Urgent as immediate losses.

I tear pages out of notes to myself.
Make small loans to my imagination.
When I listen to the silence, to the silence
When I listen to the silence, the silence
All that is mixed, focused, unfocused…
All my lovers stroll through with their
Elusive pride grown together, with love-
Making reduced to sweet moments and my
Blood fires tell me a thing or two about
My sources. I can't find them otherwise. I
Reach out saying so what back to the room,
Put off what I am supposed to do and
Tell myself stories about the source
Of the winds. Dreaming
And not dreaming. I push them together
With my hands. They coalesce.

MOUTHFUL OF DREAMS

Mouthful of dreams
Pulling on your head
To make it ring like a bell.

Suddenly, you're singing.
Suddenly, your breath is news.
Sounds like this:

Kiss me, kiss me, kiss me,
Kiss me, kiss me, kiss me.

There's a light far away
In the forest.
Let's dance over there
To every song we sing.
So we sing every song we know
To bring their choirs close,
To notice every angel
Oh see the flashing of their wings.

The voice of every angel
Clings to every song we sing.
So we sing every song we know
To bring their choirs close,
To see the flashing of their wings.

WEDDING POEM
(For Sandra y Geoff)

From Izalco, the lighthouse,
A great song began.
The red tiles of the roofs reflected
This song and sent it high
Above San Salvador,
High above San Miguel and Santa Ana.
Beyond Chalatenango and Jutiapa.
San Antonio de Cortes y San Pedro Sula,
High above the fire mountains,
Over the hills full of coffee,
Far beyond the bancos worried
About Colons and dollars.

For a long time the song was lost
In the crazy air over
The Gulf of Fonseca. Slowly
It found its way to El Norte.

The old gods watch the people of Salvador,
Wishing them happiness, great and lasting,
The song found its way into one
Heart, then another, until the song
Became the heart of Salvador.

It sings in every one of its people.
It is not a song of words,
But of love, so that all
May understand it. Sandra
Sings this song to Geoff and Geoff
Hears Izalco's song, sees the fire
In her eyes, knows how pure
The song of love can be.

They become one song.
The singing never stops.
The volcanoes of El Salvador
Glow red against the night
Like the lips of lovers singing
To each other, on and on forever.

A SMALL TRINKET HELD TO THE SUN

There is a point where I
Brushed a picture of you across
My mind. A landscape near the sea.
Unable to bring the islands
Into focus, I called upon the weather.
Moisture in the air, a discrepancy of temperature
Between the forms of water. Captured
Here, a moment of the heart; alone,
Unaccustomed to such luxury it
Speaks aloud. "I love you," it says.

We traveled from Paris to Barcelona,
Giving gray to blue, as easily as kisses
Between friends. The sunlight on
Your face, a certain music in your voice.

In the sky tram above the harbor,
We saw Columbus pointing up Las Ramblas.
"I'll make up a story about our being here,"
I promised. What would happen?

Now November closes door after door, trying
To end the year as graciously as possible.
I hold you in my arms before you go
To sleep tonight. The Leonid meteor
Shower blasts through us; little holes
In every fabric, all unnoticed.

Another song begins, despite the hour.
I listen to it carefully. We rain into each other.
High above this place, we flash signal after signal.

NOW THAT YOU ARE FINALLY HERE

We must make this as brief
As possible. Many others have been
Here before you. Look for their signs.

There is much you might come to know.
Everything moves in cyclic patterns.
Do not get used to this, so that
All becomes indistinguishable, one
Morning, the same as another. The night
Pulsing over and over is not the same
Song. Please do not come to believe
In boredom, in a false sameness.

We know nothing well. All of the earth
Moves as constantly as the weather.
Love as much as you are able to:
Animals, rain storms, great
Tragedy, great adventure, great memory,
Each other, the stars, your self.

Go back to what you were doing.
Put these words where you might find them again.
Read this poem once more. Pretend that you said
These things. Tell others to do so, too.

GRACE

SOME FAIRIES

The fairy of the heart.
The fairy of memories.
The fairy of autumn nights.
The fairy of the end of childhood.
The fairy guarding the feet of travelers.
The fairy who can speak the spells of olden times.
The fairy who can know when love is true.
The fairy of the evening summer grass.
The fairy of the fireflies.
The fairy of secret places.
The fairy who is seen but once.
The fairy who watches sleep descend.
The fairy of the Spring dances.
The fairy of long friendships.
The fairy who chases loneliness.
The fairy who appoints the stars.
The fairy who reveals what was hidden.
The fairy who can see lost things.
The fairy who protects the smallest breezes.
The frost fairy.
The fairy of winter windows.
The fairy who protects enchantment.
The fairy of distant music.
The fairy at the doors of dreaming.
The fairy called "delight of the newborn."
The fairy who attends the songbirds.
The fairy who can weave with music.
The fairy of the garments of the seasons.
The fairy lit by moonlight alone.
The fairy of the storm.
The fairy from the bows of ships.
The fairy of the starlit meadows.
The fairy of the grace in language.

GRACE

First we noticed places within
The room where there was no presence
Of sound at all. Pools of stillness.

They seemed to move from location
To location. When we ran across
The room quickly, sound stopped
And started as we moved through
Them. This was not all.

The sounds changed when one
Passed through these spaces.
A conversation might become
A speech about opera or a scream.

Often we heard music of a curious
Kind and other times animal sounds.
Waterfalls, sirens, myriad of languages,
Fog horns in the distance, secrets being
Told. It became difficult to cross the room.

As we came to understand that life
Here was not linear in any fashion
Save a period of consciousness,
Then a period of unconsciousness,
We realized that these sounds could
Become more graceful, that one could
Stand in these sound pools for long
Periods; come to realize ideas, music,
The way the weaving went with sense.

Now we look for the places where
The sound ceases for a time; where
We can sit without its insistence,
Watching the spaces it occupies
Open and close, open and close,
Finding the music occasionally,
Finding the small spaces within

The melody, the room switching
Identity, negative to positive.

Which were the holes of sound?
Which were the realms of silence?
How did we come to perceive them?

CESAR CHAVEZ SWOOPS DOWN

There were thousands of people at the gate
When you came through. We knew it was you.
A streak of light, a brilliant blue
And a quietness that was like
Watching waves at neap tide, a rolling
Made understandable by the way
The water breathed around us.

We began receiving signals early on.
We were told that everyone who ever
Loved anyone was now on line speaking
To one another. Communication beyond all odds.

"Hey, girl, I love you" tat, tat,
"Hey boy, where are you? I love you too."
Fields of electricity slicing the night like
Bad feelings. "We can't talk this way
Again. I must have you in my arms
In order to say anything to you."

You are talking to flocks of birds.
You are talking to the ripped edges of dreams,
Undone before the dawn and without any knowledge
Of arms around each other, of songs that spoke to your
mother.

From the fields comes a high humming.
It is all of the hearts together, all of the loved ones
Who pick these crops, who pull the clumps of grapes from
The vine. They are one voice now.

Mis Amigos, mi Corazon
From the middle of the heart
De medio Corazon
A larger song, the humming continues.

Ahora estoy con tigo.
Miren hace a ustedes. Ellos son nostros.

DREAM FLYING AROUND THE ROOM WITH A PIECE OF STRING STILL ATTACHED TO IT, JUST AS I WOKE UP

"The fireflies are spelling out your name."
"Well, it's spelled just like it sounds."
"Fireflies hear things differently than us."
"I guess so. They do have their own music."
"What does it sound like?"
"It's kind of a clicking and buzzing."
"Do they dance to it?"
"Of course."
"They must be good with words. There it is again."
"Is this a common occurrence?"
"No, it's hard to get everyone together."
"I've been coming to this place my entire life."
"So have they."
"It's so magical. Smell the air."
"Mmmmmmm… What is that scent?"
"Memories. I think it is memories, anyway."
"They have a scent when they aren't connected to anything specific."
"How do you know that?"
"I dunno, read it somewhere, I guess. I forget where."
"Listen — a bird is singing itself to sleep."
"Sometimes in Summer they do that all night."
"I wonder why?"
"I think they like the way it sounds. That's enough."
"It almost seems unreal."
"These things always do."
"I'm glad we're here."
"That's the idea."
"And alive. And in love."
"Mmmmmm. Mmmmm."
"I used to think we'd have to make up places like this."
"Later on we will."
"What do you mean?"
"Recalling things. It's like watching a fire flicker."
"There's the wishing star."
"Where?"

"Just above the lake."
"What happens when wishes don't come true?"
"Oh, they wiggle their way into songs sometimes…and sun-
sets."
"I think some of them come back to get wished again."
"I'm sure they do."

THE RINGS OF BEAUTY

They have their own
Vistas, uncomplicated,
Stark and sustained
By music understood
Implicitly when
The deep heart's core
Seeks to embrace
A particular calling;

A calling not so much
Memory as a strident
Insistence that compels
One to gaze for decades
Over a painting, or
Repeat the words of a
Poem throughout a lifetime,
As if all of creation
Depended upon it.

Paris embraces Helen,
Odysseus, Penelope,
Chopin, Madame Sand;
The Schumanns dance together
Before the hearth,
Joyce watches the chimneys of Dublin.
Pound engages myriad Chinese women
While dreaming of Dante's mouth
Teasing that of Beatrice;
Mann boards a Berlin trolley,
Noticing the weather, so particular
Today; Callas, standing at the seaport,
Whispering to Monet and Bonnard,
Everyone already old.

The night declares
It's queen once again.
Stars begin to repeat
Themselves, to become
Constellations.

We walk through Paris,
Now a city, listen to
Recorded music, revel at
Monet's memory. We try
Not to look back.
Try to ignore Orpheus
Screaming as we crest
The hill, the river before
Us, no passage denied,
Ring upon ring presented,
Moment upon moment

BIG HOTEL

Down the Delta, below Courtland,
Before Walnut Grove, there used to be
A large hotel; "Came right up to
The road," said Fred, trying to recall
Its name. Burned down, nothing left
To mark it at all. No one there able
To recall that name. The river has
Its own intentions, remembers and
Forgets at will, rises and falls,
Carries everything downstream,
Trees, boats, bodies, the procession
Of days, to the Bay, then to the ocean.
It too cannot recall the names. Its
Past is all the land, its character
Any particular spot along its course
Recalled at random, collectively agreed
Upon as having some things in common
With the flow of the conversation.

FEBRUARY, UNAWARES

There seem to be small lights
In the water, just at the edge of the dock.
I've been watching them for hours.
They flick on and off, changing colors,
Making random patterns just
Below the surface. They do
Not appear to be attached to anything.
Rather, signals from below the water,
Defragmenting some larger
Information, condensing space,
Too small to be seen otherwise.

A word appears.
It is displayed briefly but
Clearly.
Again, it reads.
Then Look, quickly followed by
Time, This, Here, Changing,
Moment, Practice, Stillness.
Then Nothing.

The patterns do not return.
A number of fish gather where
These lights have been, breaking
The surface, falling back, flashing
Silver sides as they do.

I don't expect anyone to believe
This. I was alone. The place
Was remote. The evening was a quiet one.
These things happen occasionally.
We consider them wonders.
Talking lightning, a display of bio-
Luminescence, a new way to
Communicate, a privilege to observe,
To see and hear things all around us.
Knowing the night and the day.
Hurling through space on

A beautiful blue planet,
Counting all the stars as we do so.

TALKING TO DAVID AGAIN

It was like thinking.
Idea comes in, not quite
Willed but dressed for
The occasion, no matter what.

This is what we have.
This is what we want to do.
This is how beautiful it is.
This is what might happen.
This is how I am feeling.
This is who will get hurt with this action.
This is what it sounds like.

A long wind, a raven wind.
Dark hair spread across a pillow.
Lying awake listening to breathing
Beside you. Looking at the ceiling
Not thinking, then thinking again.

Thoughts are like waves.
We need not request them.
They have their own agenda,
Even if we do not act upon them.
Desire drives the car. It has no
Sense of speed or direction. It
Only makes things happen.

Later, we stand together understanding
Everything as much as possible about ourselves.
Why we acted the way we did. What we said.
What we did not say. Nor do they seem the same,
Do not make a difference. We decide that these
Shared experiences are memories. Things we
Never said to one another but felt them, mutually
Acknowledged. Looking at them with this lens
They dance brilliantly without any help from ourselves.

LEAVING THE LITTLE HOUSE

The gardens had been reduced
To three small glass globes
Filled with glycerin and white
Snowflake-like particles. I could
Still smell the marigolds.
The edges of the yard glowed
With an unsettling fluorescent
Green. The list of desires
Remained attached to the refrigerator
Door with magnets commemorating
Heroes of a fourteenth-century
Battle. Your smile refused
To vacate; hiding in boxes, corners.
The edges of the windows,
Glistening like the place was a diamond
Mine.

I pushed the car out of the garage,
Imagined the place in flames,
Drove away thinking the lawn
Needed mowing, the rain gutters cleaning.

FOR MY DAUGHTERS AS I
AM FIFTY-FIVE YEARS OLD

When I was young, before I knew you,
Octobers were twice as long and played
Their weather through the slanting
Light. I belonged to it and it to me.

When I was young, before I knew you,
Books were bright candles and stayed
Alive and true. They are still my friends,
Still there. I belong to them and they
Belong to me.

When I was young, before I knew you,
Music was a great room and made me
Pathways, roads and seas
To sail. I belonged to it and it to me.

Now, not so young, I do know you
And you are love that doesn't fade.
And I am new with all the gifts
That love can bring. I give
These gifts to you and you
Give them back to me.

A CHANGE IN THE WEATHER
(For Alison Greenberg)

I kept thinking there would be
More time, or that someone nearby
Would suddenly burst into a song
So beautiful that everyone would
No longer be afraid, or hungry,
Pure hearts shining, a good song.
I kept thinking that there would
Be a sign, at least a sign.

The night is greasy.
Sometimes I can't sleep. The children
Are growing so quickly. They learn
About the world. I try to help them.

The stars are breathtaking. Just look
At them. And I have friends, real
Friends. Often we go outside together,
At night, to watch and listen to the hissing
Of the stars. It is grand.

There is enough time. There is
A song. The children come with
Us. Occasionally it rains.
We can hear the wind in the trees.
To each other we say: "I love you."
Thunder rolls through the air, through
Our bodies. A sign, surely a sign of some kind.
Isn't it?

PRIVATE ARCHÆOLOGY

TOWN OF NIAGARA – LATE 1940'S

Here is where the railroad tore
Through the edge of our town.
Black earth, black air and the perfect
Angel, steam, sung by whistle
Toots and a language of flags,
Brakemen's lanterns and the booming
Freight cars tearing dark holes
Through all the seasons.

We were Town of Niagara boys.
The city boys knew it because
We walked in the streets when
We crossed Hyde Park bridge
To go into the city together.
We didn't have sidewalks.

Our barber shop in a drear
Apartment building called
The Ten Commandments.
Mr. Brunetti's grocery store,
Where he reigned, cigar mashed
In his face, his wife, small,
Watching from the shadows.

Brownie's gas station "If you can't
Come in smile as you go by", the sign
Facing cobblestones of Hyde Park
Blvd. There was a war in Europe,
Japan. It seemed exotic until
The dead came home and we
Knew their names and faces,
Their mothers and fathers.
The flag-draped boxes and crisp
Ceremony. Taps at Riverdale.
It was good to be from there.
Where the air always smelled.
Chemicals and hot slag in the night
Poured into open fields from

Midnight trams, glowing as our
Lives glowed, brighter than radio
Dials tuned to the news and spoken
Fictions churning it all together.

The town, the trains, the Ten
Commandments, the cigar, the dull
Gas station and nights filled
With the crazy wonder of it all.

HORSES AT THE EDGE OF THE SEA

The horizon is far away, a sullen
Fog, a brooding and endless grey,
Begrudging the evening light,

Holding it for minutes then allowing
A spot of sun, red light on waves. It dapples
The hides of the horses, then quickly
Excuses itself and wanders up to the sand cliffs and gets lost
In the canyon leading to the water.

There is a stillness to all this.
The sound of air in and out
Of horse nostrils. A shiver
Across the back, small pawing
On the sand.

Somewhere a bird knows something
About all of this and makes its special noise.
Eyes roll toward the sound then back
To the edge of the water.

The horses are seemingly doing nothing.
They have come down here for the evening, as
We do, without expectations or purpose
Beyond just being there at that moment.

We watch them grow darker in the fading
Light until they are shadow forms against
A sea moving back and forth on the edge.

Now there is land. Now there is water.
Now there is light. Now there are horses.
Now there is nothing to see.

BLANKET

A drifting in the heart. Long
Sounds that find no solace. No matter
Where they go they remain wanderers.

We will find them on the shores of the lake
After storms that rip the lining of the night
Easily from its darling moon.

Someone must have seen where the careful
Touch has gone, where the sandals cut
The crust of the morning away from the bread
And no hand, oh pretty creatures they are,
could move, move as brutally, tearing the stars
Down from the black lion of night,
All kindness gone, its blue cart tipped
On its side in the crowded streets.

No one wonders any longer
Dammit all anyway. All they ever
Wanted were blankets to keep warm
And just a touch of a hand,
Someone to say, "Do not be afraid at all."

NO MIRROR

I thought I spoke to you.
I thought you were in the room,
That there was religion in
There with you, a melting into a wall,
Something divine that we would
Have no control over.

And indeed, it was everything
That was not you. I could hear
You weeping as you walked along
The beach trying so hard to be
A monk, anything holy.

I thought I could feel you
Touching me and that you made me think of
You naked and moving over my body,
Except my thoughts could find
No mirror, there was no laughter,
Just the clicking as the wind moved
The door slightly open, then slightly
Closed, almost aimlessly with
The rule being we were to notice
The differences and make something
Deep and important of it all.

THE CERTAIN STILLNESS OF THE SKY

Lost in the waltz, the wind skirls briefly,
Opening the morning hours toward ten
O'clock and examines the branches of the trees
Almost as if it were inspecting every leaf.
The trees shutter and toss their crowns
Back and forth across what may be real
Music after all.

There have been the clouds, every day
For weeks now, mountains of them,
Never tired, constantly flying by, excited
By the air and how the sky holds them,
Letting them be free, but still, in its blue
Dream of atmosphere.

There was a chalice suspended
In the air tonight. It glowed with
Silver light and the moon rose
Just above it and centered itself
Over the cup. The animals dropped
To their knees and the barnyard
Was still for a time except for crickets
Singing to one another. It was lovely
And had never happened before.

Now, wandering the hills in this moonlight,
I find myself at the base of an oak tree.
The grass in this place has been cropped
By sheep for one hundred years.

Except for the hiss and pop of the night
As it rises to the moonlight in an erotic
Dance, I can remember little except
For saying, "Hello hills. Hello moon.
Hello trees and hello" to this huge

Stillness as I press myself deep into
The earth pretending I too am planted
Here, hard against this night, able only
To give praise, "Hallelujah, Hallelujah."

THE FAR LORDS

The days of dream.

Those tiny rooms we can gaze
Into but are forever unable to reach
As much as a finger length into
To see if it is real or not.

A gull running along the shoreline
Dragging a wing staring at the sea.
There is no sound on earth breaking
Like these waves. The evening eats,
Dines on everything and smiles
Back at us, content that
We are there, helpless yet
Full of understanding.

I'm sorry. I am unable to speak
To you like this any longer.
It is nothing personal. It is a
Fault of suddenly noticing that
curtains surrounded every room.

And then there is that cat meowing
Just out of sight, in the dark
Sounding like it wants to get in,
If just for a minute.

TRANCE WALKING

A certain blindness catching
One unaware and without guile,
A shuttering hurries into the room
Lodging in the darker corners
As if observing something that
Prompts enchantment, a peculiar
Green light perhaps, moving in
Patterned ways as it begins to describe
A series of motions, almost a language,
But one that has been forgotten
For a long time by all but scholars.

Soon different cities begin to appear.
One does not know the names of these
Places yet still they seem familiar,
The patterns of lights, the way they blink
Off and on requiring attention and careful
Observation as if one were expected
To know what these places were,
Why we should see them now,
Why we would feel as if we were
Walking near them feeling
Inches off the ground so no sensation
Of the ground beneath the feet would
Be felt. An unstopping and constant
Pace across the night, knowing always where
The next step would take one.

It is possible in doing this to visit
All the shrines of the Buddha
If we do it consciously
But we do not. We float through,
Stranded in our dreams, looking
From our bodies at the landscapes

Skipping by, believing we are traveling
To destinations we have yet to learn
The names of, islands perhaps,

Jungles and vast deserts, but we
Are not. We are trance walking,
Trying to force ourselves awake, going
Into the kitchen to make a cup of tea,
Glancing out the window and seeing
The moon for the very first time.

CIRCUMSTANCES

Traveling back and forth between
The woods and the edge of the river
I had never tried to understand much
Of what I encountered. It made everything
More dream-like and the days and evenings
More beautiful as if I were a child
Once again and all was not
Carried like blood being transported
To a situation requiring it for life.

There is always so much indecision
As if we wait for someone we hardly know
To tell us what is actually happening
Or later we see it in a film or video clip
Thinking it is something we truly remember.

How long this hour is, whatever it was?
There are no measures that ever are certain.
We breathe and miss our own breathing.

Everything seems strange as we live within it.
It all eventually seems senseless. There are
Always cards somewhere on the table.

We never want to speak to the circumstances.
A long silence births itself and fills with
Dark pleasure. We are sleeping side by
Side and I never saw who you were
For a long time. We will be dust.
I may say I will see you again
This way between these woods and that
Grey-green river that moves so quickly
And once again it will be circumstance.
We become instruments of it and bow.

DANCING

What, that we could look across the harbor
And still see the boat that brought us here
Steaming away like a black maggot, belching
Diesel and left over evening, splashing red and lurid
Blues all around the upper air. We would be here

Forever and we knew it. Someone lit a cigarette,
Passed it around until it was nothing as well.
We were not seeking. We weren't even saying.

It was mostly that it was cold and we were without
Features now that night had taken the brush,
Painting furiously to get ahead of a moon that
Would be pale, almost green as it tried to overcome
The entrance hymn that night had prepared.

Somewhere someone began to play an old tango,
El Amanecer, I think it was. It felt like blood coming
From a cut wrist as it inched its way closer. If we
Hadn't been so distracted by the situation we
Might have tried to forget the little bird sounds
That filled its middle, but we were unable to do so.

Better to stay huddled here, away from all
Conversation, dedicating ourselves to leaving
Rather than looking for Albion. Pierre suggested
We try to dance. I took a long drink and stood up.
"Two-step or waltz, tango or polka?" I bowed to everyone
Gathered there in the black and imagined they did so as well.

CAPES AND CLOTHING

She puts on the cape of swans.
She puts on the cape of darkness.
She puts on the cape of dim music.
She puts on the whispering cape.

She has the songs already in the chamber
When she fires. They look for corners
In the night where they may hide as darkling beetles
Do. She puts on the chorus of stridulations.

It is so easy to be distracted, to look away,
To lose sight of her movements. She wants
It that way and drives her car as if it were
A moth finally escaped from the flame charms.

The sea horns begin to make their low pitched
Bellows. "There are dangerous rocks here",
They announce without any words at all.
Everyone cowers in fear, the sound of the waves

Crashing against the cliffside. Let us hurry.
Bring the instruments. Find where the words
Are kept, what shapes may be noticed in deepest
Night, where the moon is resting right now.

She puts on the hood of stars.
She puts on the shoes of the sylph-footed.
She makes the gestures learned from the old days.
She slips away before we ever get near her.

THE WOLF THAT BELONGS TO TIME

You are not the ocean
And I am not a sailor
But I've spent my life at sea
And meaning may escape me
But nuance never does.

I can wear music like a glove.
I can wear even deeper dress then,
In the name of love and walk with those
Sailors across the feckless path that wind
Uses to tear the edges of the land,
The edges of the soul like windows taped
Against the coming storm. We can stand
Watching glassy-eyed but keen as blades
Leaning on the sheets before the wind.

This is our ocean. I will speak to you
In the language of the sea and you
Will understand it as the voices of all
Those upon the earth who used the water
To hold their nerves and muscles,
Tissue and bones together look out from
Watery eyes across watery mornings of drifting
Rain. And I will hold you there becoming
Only another day in your life when something

Extraordinary happened and we discovered
Desire alone on the high places
Announcing the end of all waters
And saw it listened to by thousands
Of non-sailors like ourselves carrying
Our cargos of ginger and of nutmegs,
Of bolts of fine cloth and raisins
Yellow as the sun, exchanging them
With one another, trading memories

Of this time back and forth
Until the wolf of time itself comes into

Our bazaar and leans against our flesh
Again. "How is this possible?"
We all say of this great wolf.

It is immense and faceted as diamond is.
It holds our names within the great
Confusion of the days and asks a
Thousand times a day,
"Can you feel it brother?
Are you speaking? Is this our spirit
That makes me howl aloud this way?"

NORTHERN LIGHTS

You can't just throw it away. It's
Not like a morning on the water in the
West Indies, the glide of white and gray
Gulls across the small harbor, the air
Easy on the skin, a perfection of clear
Water. It is more like the night

Sky trying to hold all those stars,
Keep them in the right order and still
Convey the information of constellations,
Ancient stories and ships sharing the
Points of light to get from one place
To another. I will forget my way

Home eventually. Tracks in the snow, some
Kind of animal. Endless white
Plains. Fumbling through it looking
For a campfire, remembering a conversation
Not realizing the importance of it all,
Until the Northern Lights start up
Totally unannounced.

NIGHT SONGS

Here in these places above
The sea, it is often possible
To hear the many messages
Borne upon the winds.

While all wind is only air
Passing across a surface,
Without regard for consciousness,
On occasion one may discern
Certain sonic vibrations that may
Evidence themselves as language.

On a given day, there may be
Songs of Summer, or a telling
How trees came to have such
Irresistible glamour and presence.
At other times, long, mournful
Exclamations that drill into
The heart. Great winds may

Force one indoors where
Exclamations find voice in woodwork,
Door jambs, spaces between window
And sash, between shingles or loose
Pieces of metal flashing upon a roof.

Some would not consider this to be
Language. Consider then, how music
Changes through the ages, how certain
Sounds become part of its making.
Also how all words come and go in
Our discourse from age to age and are
Renewed or lost as time becomes its
Own wind. Then listen once again

To a description of a Summer night
As proclaimed by breezes in the screen,
How certain periods of silence may

Change the meaning of the moment
Again and then again, how these
Words whirl through your mind,
A fluttering like a flame in air,
A language seeking understanding there.

DOME

It looked like the dome of heaven
Had shattered and come down
Around her. She sat in the middle
Of the room kind of smiling, kind
Of crying but mostly not wanting
To be there at all. There was no

Reason to sing a song but
She did and it was full.
The sun going down inside the words,
Cracking night open and there still
Wasn't anyone coming.

She watched her horse shiver
As the light failed and once
Again she was alone and trying
To make sense of anything that had
Happened over the past few days.

In the distance light was leaking
Through a yellow window shade.
She was speaking to herself,
Wanted to go toward it
As if it could be a comfort, but
It flashed out. The dark
Surrounded her, sooty,
Crude, final and somehow hurt
That not even a candle would stay
Lit to help define it being night.

She stopped singing and flew
To a high corner of the room
Just as an angel would do
Given half a chance with that crowd.

I watched her walk back toward
Her car, start it and drive away.
Pain didn't have enough of itself
To keep her any closer and all
That sparkling and all those perfect chords
Were just a song after all.

DRY ROCK STAIRCASE

These roses in a row were planted
So long ago it is almost impossible
To tell there was once a house here.

I came upon them while traipsing
Through the drying fields and wondering
At the open space close to the creek.

They seemed out of place. Why would
roses choose to be here red, yellow
And a fiery orange, rangy but quite
Lovely? I paced the area and realized
A house had been there about a hundred
Or so years previously. This was the back
Garden. Then, at creek edge
A lilac full of the season.
This was a home, no doubt.

I sat on a rock for the afternoon
Watching the slow turning of the turkey
Vultures, listening to the landscape,
Imaging the seasons, a dry rock
Staircase leading to a dancing floor
Once full of life, now brushed
By ghosts and the fine voices of insects
Tidying up the Summer as their own house.

DAYLIGHT'S PURIFYING SKY
AT LAND'S END

We thought they were clouds
But they were not clouds at all,
Marching just above the sea.
They were the souls of miners
Finally set free to walk the coast
Once again; the grey of fog,
The sting of salt water on their faces
Washing the coal, the metals away.

We cannot dream these things.
They come like unwelcome family
To live with us and we cannot
Refuse their entrance.

The foghorns keen across
That last of land. We cannot
See the stars tonight. We never
Imagined things would turn
Out this way, leaning on our picks.

THE POEM

The poem was coming from far
Across the hills. I could see
The riders with their dust of words,
Phrases and half-heard conversations.

The stories unpacked and fluttering.
The packages of winds and words all shuttering,
As I lay beneath the trees muttering
And I was trying to breathe.

It would wind in close and say
Things to me that I knew were true
But would never happen,
Could never happen,
To either me or you.

Close up, one could smell the horses,
See the foam upon their lips
And catch a glimpse of the riders,
Only the briefest glimpse of the riders
And their shining eyes.

Then gone, completely gone.
No bird sounds or hush of insect feet,
No drifts of stars or sense of night
Or day. The wave uncurled
Completely and took the poem away.

THE IMMORTAL

I had a dream but it was not
My own, but part the tossed-off
skin and jumbled bones of
Another's vision, an unknown home,

A further coming of the night
Into my sleep, gathered from an
Immortality not mine yet
Not an accident, a circumstance

Where one who has abandoned
Time or time abandoned one
Became a universal history, where
Our very blood inherits music
Or reflections from another childhood

Saying a phrase that waters the living
With the cast-off moments of one
Long ago alive, who is now
Completely unknown to them

Slips quite easily into
The form of dreams finding itself
Flabbergasted again in a life
And is worn again as poetry might be,
A garment, a forgotten country, a tree.

THE PIPER

Water on our lips. We look for
The sake of looking and are happy.
Now in the valley we watch the moon
Creep into a delicate sky.

Tonight it is round and pale
And full of the unfolding one finds
In the harness of what we choose
To call loving. Smiling at the
Minotaur, knowing it will not
Be remembered in the morning,
We have said goodbye to this
Mind so long ago we can dance
In forgetting what is past.
It hurries by and we will only watch.

All the sound of water here
Again. All of the books that have
Been written, destroyed and are
Here again. We have rewritten
Each and every one of them. The ink
Made of the carbon of our bodies.
The ink made of our blood and the blood
Of soldiers in endless armies.

There are no longer any secrets.
When you whisper in my ear
The cyclone blows across the pampas
And the dry deserts, across the
Dry husks where love used to live,
Lifting its perfect dust until
It is impossible to see the sun at all.

PRIVATE ARCHÆOLOGY

There was a theodicy
In the way she spoke,
An argot balanced in
A semantic wind that
Keeps us from understanding
Almost anything she says.

"The meaning is 'elusive'"
She explains, "like polyphony.
It is linked and unlinked,
Tied and untied but still
Able to double as a compass
Or an algebra of groups and tensors
Stumbling over each other in an attempt
To get something said perfectly or not
Said at all but hammered into
The stomach, a broken mirror
At best, concealed but
Retrievable only through
A private archælogy."

"This is an architecture," she continues,
"But not a cathedral at all."

*
**

"What you need is a cup of coffee
And a walk in the park. You've
Made a mess of trying to talk to one
And all. Try kissing me on the lips
Right now and see if it could
Possibly help you." Then the fire
Engines started up and she
Was gone again, worshipping
All of language like a riot in a church.

DINNER TIME

No one has used this road since
The end of World War II when
Rain came down for eight days
Drowning the wood, abandoning
Even the golden voices of the animals
That once lived here.

It wasn't that it was dark,
Thoughts could easily become more dense
Than the crippled light that insisted
On being there despite having been foreclosed
And locked with thorns that seemed
Sharper than memory when unfolded.

But we came here anyway, if only
To be troubled by the fact that the road
Refused to go away or stop leading
To anywhere; a cut where, looking ahead
One could see the trees break and an open
Meadow lean ahead all the way to the lake
Shore. In the summer there were fireflies
That received the place like a memory.
Summer is gone, the war is gone
And we, for want of learning something special,

Something to place at the service of trying
To understand all the histories all over again,
Caused us to falter a bit and look
Cautiously about us to see if we could
Explain anything about this loss or the place
Itself that might leave us feeling
Intrusive about our need to be here.
The placid shadows, the mothers calling
Their sons home to dinner across the fields.

CHANTING

I woke up in hell and did not
Recognize it at all. This must
Be a dream. The edges of the room
Curling slightly. The blur the objects
In the room had when one looked
Directly at them made the same noise
Lucid dreaming does as it empties us

Or contains us in that special way we
Recall upon waking. This place was
A neighborhood and I was compelled
To search my pockets. I felt I must
Deliver some serious message. I was
Confused. I did not know the why of
Anything I found myself concerned with.

I put my feet on the floor. I was
Growing fear as if it could be harvested.
This was dissolute. I must be here forever.

I woke up trembling.
I could hear the faraway sounds
Coming from the chapel. The monks
Were singing in Latin, call and response.

I was visiting this place. Hell was
A course of action left over from
Some reading about an argument.

I listened to the chanting for as long
As I was able. Gradually clusters of angels
Began to promenade and seek color.

LIFEBOAT

We were looking out the window
Toward the sea. There was one
Tree on the left at the edge
Where the cliff dropped off
Bringing the blue light into
The room and carefully placing
It on the few pieces of furniture.

There is a forward motion that
Takes your entire life to understand
Or begin to understand, when the words
Find their own power and there is no
Deliberation any longer. One may
Not know where they are going
But the perfection is both pure and lonely.

We would stand here for a long time.
I would watch the light change in your eyes.
I would make up stories to myself
That had absolutely no words, just
Sensations sliding over my nerves,
Lapping at the synapses, sparkling
At the crispness our breathing could be,
Loving how the rest finally comes.

GIFTS OF THE WIND

She filled the evening
With a quiet song that
Made me put my head
Against the earth and close
My eyes as if I were very much
In love and very much alone
At the same time.

Soon other voices joined hers
And the sky grew darker.
I could hear kalimbas being
Played far away. They sounded
Like birds might sound when they
Realize they are dancing.

THE FINE CHALICE OF LARRIN

Whomever it was kept the moon
In that glass casket for such
A time as he did was finally
Convinced by the sight of the cup
Held by the glittering watchers of Larrin,
To give it up and put it back
To work the tides and pull
The heart strings of so many who
Dwell in the realms near
The Isles of Fog and Challenge.

How was this cup to have
Such power? How was the mere
Sight of its quiet grace to move
Such power to reach inside
And pluck the fair moon
With its light, paler than the voices
Lovers use when they keep the birds
At their whispered secrets calm,
Then release them to the night
To carry ships of dreams into
The lands beyond the woods?

We are a kin to twilight
In that beauty is illusive.
We are driftwood from far
Away islands come here to
Make the stuff of legends,
Fabulous songs anchored
Within us as if we were as
Substantial as temples,
Not mere acquaintances of a laughing
Wind, just ahead of the morning,
Just ahead of lightning.

We are asked to bring such
Things as the Fine Chalice of Larrin
As if it were some kind of song
Remembered by survivors of mythical
Wars or brothers and sisters to those
Who walked out of the dark
Splashing toward the sunrise full
Of their golden mist. We are required
To waken these stories, bringing amazing
Beauty to all. We are required to be
Divine, more mystical than women
Are mystical and offer this deathless
Chalice to those who believe in how
Words themselves can equal the greatest
Secrets without ever guessing their meaning.

A LIMITED MEANS
OF EXPRESSION

PROLOGUE

A TRAVELER'S TALE

In the blood of evening we wade
Through the moments listening for thunder,
Something we can rely on before we wash
Our legs to get ready for the night.

I do not understand why we continue
To reach for one another but I do
Participate. Perhaps it is for the feel
A hand might have touching near the heart,
Asking a forgiveness that is non-specific
But well meant, wanting something to be
Done before the whole place becomes
Dark and we stumble from one pool
Of light to another never sure our direction
Is correct or even necessary, before
It gets too dark to see your eyes

Before me. Perhaps we will be in love.
Perhaps we will find a doorway for a
Moment, crouch there and begin to relate
Stories to each other as if it were
Important for us to hear them.

I will tell you how I came here
Across the wine dark sea of ancient
Time and found myself just outside the city
At this time of day, traveling with
the others past the dim orchards,
Seeing the fires on the horizon, hoping
Rest would be full of peace, quiet
Song and the precious company
And comfort one might find here.

It seems a long way to travel
To find only the bloody failing
the light is intent on illuminating.

We begin to call to one another,
Softly at first, then louder
Always trying to make the new
Distinctive, luxurious to discuss
And comely in its transformation,
Its shading, its interlocked devices,
Our commerce in its patterns, always new,
Always skillful, filled with a fragrance
Unbound by the finality of daylight,
Praying we may never be so totally alone.

1. LIMITED MEANS

THE VANISHING

It began with the wind.
It always is the wind.
It is that voice that moves
Through our clothing and over
Our skin as if it has always
Known us intimately. We are

Without defenses. We wait for it.
Then the light. God, the light.
How does it do that across the
Landscape and into form even
As we look toward anything?

It just kept getting brighter
Every second until we could no
Longer see. We were part of light
At last, moving in waves within
Each other, permeable in ways
We did not understand. It was

Here that everything vanished, Everything
Vanished. Everything. We could hear
The larger animals and the insect voices,
The music of the spheres and the
Celebrations of a million children
All drawn here to watch it all
Go away. We should be as blind,

We should have known this would happen.
We would think it a spectacular part
Of life, but it was a vanishing,
Complete and surprising, unexpected
As millions of gallons of crude
Oil erupting from the sea floor,
Covering all of a large gulf of
Water with vanished life.

LAMENTATIONS

A wandering of the spirit
Clothed like an idiot
In the worst weather, issuing
Sounds that take the heart
Away slowly so one can watch
It leaving through the filtered
Light of the jungle,
Past a small clearing then
Disappearing for a lifetime.

One becomes attached to
Living this way only because
There is little else one can call
Life but the high cries
From the canopy of night.
A Rustling of wings, some beast
Coughing into an even darker
Front where everything must
Be carried away by strangers.

We call loudly for our family,
Our brothers and sisters and the dark
Answers with measured howls and shrieking
They move the soul away from the body,

Expand everything we know toward
A false dawn or a golden moment late
In the day, evening in the mouth
Like rust, teeth clenched trying
To wake the moon to see
If it makes any sense at all;

Elemental traveling such as this,
The things we never get used to doing.

THE CHARRING

These were supposed to be lips
But have failed miserably and cannot
Offer comfort or satisfaction in any form
We can understand. The blear of sounds
Escaping from them easily becomes
Deafening without anything worthwhile
Being said. I offer you my arm instead, or
My tongue, my back, or my leg but
It will be meaningless to anyone
But those who char our knowledge.

This is like Fado when the heart
Breaks while we watch it. Here time
Unwinds directly in front of us, fills
Our eyes and handles our feelings like laundry.

We mouth the words of the charring song.
It has our family embedded in the way
We work the words. We can see deeply
Into the pool and there is no cessation
Of compassion and darker sorrow.
We overhear the Buddha on the edge
Of awakening, the last wash of
Desire stares back at him, missing him already.

SPANISH RIDERS AND GHOST LANGUAGE

The quietest of gestures, spinning
Yard after yard of silk, trying to mount
The sky, feigning indifference or instinct,

The rooms open up one into another.
Here, the entrance to an ant colony
Here, the quick rush of water as it becomes
The edge of the sea, here, the placing of
Eggs in the larvae of an entire civilization
Without its knowledge. A fog of misinformation
Clouds over the country. No one is able
To understand what anyone else means.

Battles begin. Electricity becomes visible
Whenever one takes a step, crackling beneath
The feet, sending its delicious messages
Deep into the inner core. We learn to swim
Within these momentary caverns and jagged roads.

We can never begin again. For eons we have
Been riding down and still we are unable
To recognize the Saint Elmo's fire in our fingertips.
We come to believe we are candles and trust
Many others will come to see our light, Spanish
Riders armed with ghost languages eager to
Offer recommendations and gesticulations
Deep within the social webwork where we live.

I WOULD MAKE NOISES DEEP

In my throat that sounded
So unlike anything I knew
That I would scare myself.

I became ceremony in sound.
A whirl of phlegm, crackling
And sputtering up from the
Rooms I guard against time
And her dancing princesses.

A quaking, as if a bear suddenly
Came into the room on hind
Legs and performed the crushing
Of an arm as if it were a
Dance and she the music.

Now, as autumn pushes clouds
Ahead of itself with a yard
Full of leaves, I hear these
Same sounds again issue
From their scraping across
The drive and think them
A familiar music, something
Treasured, like a Nocturne by
Chopin remembered by the fingers
Long after the mind has forgotten
The specificity of the notes and rests.
It is a rustling of lace
In a room draped with silences.

THE NIGHT PARADE

There is a kindness in watching the fires
Coming down the street carried by so many
Men dressed in radiant plumage and terse
Straps wrapped around their body.

They carry the lights high above them
On long poles so they swing to and from
As they go through their series of routines
That mean nothing to us but seem to reflect
A solidarity among these men.

The people without clothing follow in the
Shadowy darks punctuated only by flares from
Lighters used to fire cigarettes. They show lips,
The form of a hairdo, the lurid makeup of evening,
A smear on the mascara the night wears to
Prove it is beautiful. There is so much more.

The dead move through these ranks and files,
Streaming through the air, dangling their shrouds
Behind them, sweeping and looping over our heads,
Silent in their endless forward press to escape dawn.

From the top of the buildings we watch this night
Parade, thinking is must have some profound
Meaning connected to it and discover nothing
Of the kind, just shape shifting and the sound
Of heavy garments against the ground, a dim
But profound gathering that mounts the back of night
To declare its property before all light ceases and
Before the moon can shake free of clouds and rise
With book after book of sweet tales and fears,
Tides and trysts, longing and fulfillment
Learned only in her pale reflected light.

SOMETHING MORE PROBABLE

This poem is broken. I found
It that way, beyond words to fix it.
It was too complex to keep in the mind
Without something untold happening
Just as the words were to reveal
Atmospheres or a startling journey
From which no one could return without
Their entire meaning excluded or compromised.

Passages, contradictions, abnormalities
That were once thought to make it
Possible, now all exceptions to whatever
Reality and deep feeling the poem had.

Now it does not matter what direction
We choose to follow. The poem will
Have already been there before us
Using meaning as some kind of trick
That actually steals imagination away
From us, giving it to something more probable.

MAKING YOUR NAME

The wind, in from the desert,
Ruined from running through
The litany of winter, barely able
To speak. Still now, it attempts
To say your name. Blows through
The vowel sounds, leaving them
In the trees. Chases birds across
Alfalfa. Their bodies make letter forms,
Change into wheels. Unable to land
They find shelter in the ditches,
Clutching weed stalks, rocking.

Walking past the cottonwoods,
I hear it clearly for an instant,
Your name. Impossible in such
Late weather, but there, nevertheless
Or perhaps it is other, a scraping
Sound of branches against themselves,
Well above the ground. Perhaps
This is not language, this time.
Perhaps, I am wrong.

Wind inside my coat, through
The neck, forcing words from my mouth.
They make your name, as if I had
No choice, as if I were the desert,
Or, at best, a part of winter too,
Full of hands, waving, waving.

PRIVATE DANCES

Now this wind was an old one,
Gray and wandering almost
Aimlessly, disturbed at the alley,
Unwilling to find its way down there,
Barely moving the paper littered
On the ground. And that voice...

I've heard better sound on the desert,
On the sand dunes where the marks
Of bitter winds show their pictures,
Show their stories with fabled
Hands and private dances
Owned by the night and the hare
And the coyote and the soft-footed lizard.

Still, we will listen to it. It is all
We have now and we are no longer
Ourselves young. We pull our coats
Closer to our throats pretending
It is cold or relentless. It is only
Old and finally we must climb
The trees discover where it
Has come to dwell in the high branches.

TASTING THE DIRT

Not speaking the language,
I spoke in another language.

What speaks?
Does it speak for the heart?
Does it speak for time?

Is this the part of morning?

Must we always question
With desire, unhinged and hanging
Like a hook into samsara?
Will we find a mouth
In touching the edges of our dreams,
Feeling them like cloth used
To wrap the body, used to stop
The weeping, used to carry us
From loving, somehow children
Again and able to understand everything?
Will we be able to stand here with one
Another, spinning through our lives,
Fire, a metaphor, our clothing, a metaphor,
The great halls of our hearts,
A metaphor, dancing this way,
A metaphor.

Save us from other meaning,
From knowing our visions
As anything other than the singing
That they are, from the clumsy
Fabric we assemble to show
That we are the loved ones of time.

Yes, the night does come and
It is beautiful and the day too, we
Wear around us, weather, the
Reflection of all our emotions,
Clouds, our thoughts describing
The mystery of being here.
And yes, the sky is such a brilliant blue.

I shall know you forever.
There is no ground to stand that
Is not ourselves. There is no sound
That is not language. Not speaking
The language, I speak in this peculiar way,
So you may know I am among you.

WINTER LIGHT

Three trees, the only landscape.
I couldn't see past the surface
Of the water. There was a kind
Of sweet smell coming from my flesh.
The light was shattered by the afternoon.
It lay all criss-crossed on the floor,
Smashed into the door of my room and banked
Off the wrought iron bedstead.

Car skids around the corner, takes out
About three feet of fence, backs up, guns
The motor so hard it blows the muffler and
Disappears in a blast of taillights. Perhaps
It is the Winter light that makes the houses
Look so old and tired and hurt? They try
To fill themselves with the holidays, try to
Bend poor Jesus into "everything
Feeling so good." Perhaps it is just that avenue
Of trees, near the water, pretending to be
The eternal now?

When I look close at the tears in the fabric,
They seem to have been bitten through. It
Seems as if the fabric is made of so many pairs of
Old denims, plaid shirts, socks, jackets and
Navy coats with rainbow cuffs, used to grab
Big hunks of music out of time and twist them
Around guitar strings. Sometimes it is a moment
Of wind, the space before the comma, the sound of one's
Own footsteps reaching the ears. Look, over here,
Near the end of this creek, where it joins the lake,
The water seems to be making a shape, looks like
An angel. Its wings tricking against some twigs
Caught in the flood. They seem to move, then do.

A SCURRILOUS GESTURE

...thinking of J. L. Borges

Like a mouthful of broken glass
From which blood pours between the lips
with terrible panic and suffering
An audacious remark rises and thrives,
Alarmed at its own vacant worth and having been birthed
From aspersions filled with a personal holy water.

When the body was tossed into
The river I was told about it and
Believed it like a student in a
Classroom eating a peach; the most
Serious of subjects was introduced
Full of the virgin and secret treasure
Stabbed into every dream that even
Recalled what had happened that night.

The anguish was terrible. There was no
Measure as days have no measure.
I didn't fully understand until now.
The talons of sadness are a narrow pass.

These words needed a dagger. A real
Dagger as if someone had voiced
"His time had come." Oh please!
The dead are always wax no matter
How much we are fascinated by them.

We continue to tell the story
But it is only a gesture. We believe
Someone has died. When we pray

All is different. The door opens.
We see who is coming. We see the hand.
The gestures are like stab wounds.
We try to hide, begging history for any
Form at all to hide the pain.
I reach for my knife, make a scurrilous gesture.

2. THE WHITE CAVES

THE WHITE CAVES

The white caves are the imagination.
It is possible to eat your imagination,
To become the monster or the daily bread.

I am going to open my hand.
Children will be living there.
Listen carefully. They are singing.

A line of fire describes itself
Across the sky. It gives me information
About the nature of love but I am unable
To understand it. I plead with you for answers.

My life listens to God . It makes this noise
Because of that. This IS silence.

Oh there is a beautiful, tall crane standing in the rushes.
It has feathers of white and gray and of red.
It's beak spears fishes and fishes stained
With the colors of the world.

Ghosts swing their oil-filled lamps
Close to our feet and pretend to light the way.
We think we can not go on like this.
Everyday brings messages on the air.
They are full of pain and terror.

Still, no one has spoken your name.
Surely there is a good in that, mountain
Air catching at our hearts, loving creation.

What would you give to hear sounds
Like this again and again?
I will give you this alone…
Nobody wants to kill anyone else, really.

WHEN THE IMAGINATION IS UNLEASHED

There are snakes in the morning coffee.
Skin tears away from the body to become
Butterflies, candles for eyes.

Strings of lights issue forth
From the mouth. They smell
Of foreign countries and are not
Understood as language at all.

Tubes of water and ice
Burst from the ground. Entire
Rivers flow through them
Full of rapids and the winter.
They are bridges.
We walk among them amazed.
We look at our watches.
It has never been this late before.
We are tools before the beauty
Of it all.

Let us think about this.
The doors blow off everything
That was closed.
This poem becomes an exact
Copy of all that came
Before. Only the rhythm changes.

NOT A PROPHET

I'm not putting this anywhere.
I don't even know how it got here.
I was walking near dawn, the light
Became fascinating and I bent to look

Deeper into the draw near the edge of camp.
There they were, welling up on a column,
Angels, two or three. The light was so bright
It was hard to tell. And the music. i fell
To my knees. Wondered if I was praying
Or was merely impaired. At any rate, I was
Taken, completely. I was not anywhere.

I have always lived in fear. That you would
Not love me, that I would never measure up,
That what I believed in was without value
In this world. I walked tight to the ground,
Not wanting to imagine anything for fear
Of manifesting it to myself, or worse, to the world.

I took this path around the camp to the water
Supply so I would not be seen, and now these
Angels, a shaft of them whirling before me.
Everyone has seen the light leap before me.
There was no longer any hiding. I shall learn

To speak aloud, to express wonder at all,
To call out the name of the Lord in the darkness,
To be lead by this pillar all the days of my life.
I wish to speak to you. Do not deny me.
I am the one who comes to you without agenda.

DESOLATION ANGELS

The clouds open and for a moment,
Form a circle in the sky. One could
See angels moving within this circle.
Tall and pale, they are towers,
Leaning into each other and moving
Their giant wings slowly, as in breathing.

I dropped the car into a lower gear,
Swerving to avoid the back of a semi
As it exploded the road, caught up in a
Frenzy of delivery. The sky was all a gold,
A blue hole revealing a churning from
Heaven to Earth. Highway 80 West,
Aflame with the eccentricities of the early
Evening. An endless stream of vehicles
Up and down the interstate, a Jacob's
Ladder where we are all angels.

The spinning of the clouds moves,
Recedes as clouds change shape
Again. I see Sacramento in the
Distance, stringing its night lights,
Claiming the horizon. There, on
The edge of the night, it becomes
A remarkable presence. I begin to
Think that perhaps the angels dwell
There, a place of sacrament. A blue
Camaro without lights on, nearly clips
My pickup as it slides across three lanes.
Its license plate reads HLY GHST.

YOUR WINGS OF HIGH, GONE GLITTER

Sweet roads to afternoon.

I sat on the edge of the stair
And watched you come down
The fields. Long lines of you
Caught in the edges of trees.

A small hand was walking across
The top of the roses, sorting
And fumbling, like spiders when
The rain has ripped into their webs
And all the world's gone wrong
With invisible falling.

I could feel my hands moving out from my body
And go around you. I was holding you very tight.
I raised my eyes to see what to say and a star
Had somehow found its way through a space in the trees
And was sitting there watching. Sometimes it
Works like that. Sometimes I think I think it's real
And I have to stop and quiet myself, rub my eyes
To believe. It is like praying to the flowers,
Or sitting alone in the sweet roads of the afternoon
Touching your wings, gone glitter around me, listening
To the signals from the rose bushes, waiting for
Pictures to tell me how to end, quietly.

SPACE BETWEEN WORLDS

Gray angels leaning against
The door jambs. they look tired,
Not rested at all, waiting for
Some kind of dawn, a cheap
Morning they might exchange for
A burst of brightness or ethereal
Music pouring from the shadows,
Carefully gathered to impress
Those waiting for one place or another
To move to, from or toward.

Starfish, rooms filled with sea
Shells. you can't dance past that
Kind of room pal. Everything involves
A choice of some kind. We make
Very little of events that are truly
Beautiful; the long hair tumbling
Over her shoulders and the pale horses
Moving just at the edge of our understanding.
They breathe and soft while clouds of steam
Rise from their nostrils. The whole
Then is still like forgetting is still.

A flight of birds just over
The surface of the water.

ANIOLY KARTY DO GRY
(Angels Playing Cards)

There is too much light
In the room for anything irreconcilable
To happen. It will be recorded
Inside the caves, on the battlefields,

Across the purple moors and darker prairies.
The cards are flipped down upon
The table, voiceless like generations
Forced to speak to each other
Through the dark
Doors of time.

For each card is unforgiven, unforeseen
With traces in its skin of the stillness
Before birth, The Ascent of Mount Carmel,
The Olympian crucifix with its living
Christus smelling like wars and collapse
Through fire of great empires.
There is no betting at all. All blows away,
Just the open-mouthed angels constantly
Surprised at how the cards fall
As if by chance.

ANGELS AND GLACIERS

Angels in large groups are seen
Flying away from cities.
We look underneath our beds and find
Sparks of light smoldering, glints off
Silver and gold baubles left there
So they may be understood as gifts
To others, as a kind of Braille to help
Describe wonder and its patterns
Through our nervous system like
Crying children afraid to be left
This alone. We watch the angels
Depart. There is little we can do.

The glaciers have receded. So much
More land has been revealed than
We are able to understand. We are
Offered places to live, carved from stone
By huge sheets of ice. Lakes are everywhere.

There is really no place to go when
We finally realize the extent of the
Angel exodus. We look for wings, hope
We may join them, seek other ways
To understand everything that has happened.
Do you remember who I am?
Do you remember that I love you?

CHILD DANCE

Light was just coming up
As we began the dance
For fire and water together.

From this dance, steam would
Rise to the heavens, as dancers
Came together, propelled by our ritual.

First, the songs began to rise,
A verse about angel's wings,
A chorus declaring our love
For the mountains, the far
Distances, for the stilling of noises
Held by night, for the lament dealt
By those who carry time
Within their quiet appearances
Throughout their lives.
Such songs they were.

As the steam rose higher,
We knew this place, this world
Would persist past our shallow
Moments here. This was the truth.

*

It is because of this dance
That one is able to remember
Childhood, that all who dwell
Upon this earth can come and see
Time as it mixes everything into
This selfsame dance.

It is danced very seldom
For all who witnessed its
Previous incarnation must
Have passed from life before it

Could be repeated. It is
Performed with great ceremony,
The dancers consuming doubt,
Uncertainty and great fears
That all might recall this particular
Time of life. Shadows and mist.

Shadows and mist, the steps
We learn to take, the lips we
Dare to kiss. Through the fire,
Through the rain, though all
Becomes the past, we beg of grace,
Insist, that we may remember this.

MAKING WITH FRAGMENTS

for Tom Kryss

There is a moment when the lights
Become dull memories and the territories
We have come to understand in our travels
Begin to unwind and contrive their own kind
Of knowing, one coupled with the notion that

Soon an emptiness will sidle up to us and clasp
Our hand, explaining the while that we will have
Little chance of understanding emptiness and the
Damp that descends with the evening, even here

On these mountains or in this desert or along these
Trails still dusty with the echoes of elephants, ostriches,
Creatures of mystery. They will crumble, we are told
And in that moment, we believe that we are hearing
The truth rather than the banging of cymbals played
By deaf men who sold their imaginations long ago.

The multi-colored lamps make this place seem dreamed,
Not found on maps we carry, nothing promised here,
Only the trail of words that leads us on. We will recognize
Nothing but will continue so that we might see these places,
So that we may fall into the mouth of fables breathed
Over fires on some future night when the Nightjar's wings
Begin their tale and summon us from the dust once again.

I will see you there, crossing the winter night just ahead,
Betting destinies on seasons, correcting the optics
So all may see mythical beasts and believe in them
If only for the telling. Make in your mouth a story now

While you walk and breathe here that it may be told
Again at some set date far beyond these landscapes.
Favor mystery and what is lovely. Avoid the invisible
That I may feel your hand and together we will build
Toward the favoring winds, tell the dates, catch the
Glint of light on our words as they dance away from us.

UNABLE TO SAY

Do not regard it as a bad
Thing should the signs cease.

We will recognize you.
We have the seasons.
We have the weather.
The clouds will tell us much.

Watch how the light moves
Across the edges of the floor.
Indeed, it moves like flash over,
Waves of flame barely above our head.

I have some special information
For you...Can you see that glow
Coming from the mountain? It flickers
Like your own heart in a tornado.

You may be reminded of how the mind
Clicks itself off and can watch
This whole place go up in questions
About how we are even able to love one another.

The animals always move this way.
You must look for pattern: swarms
Of insects in the sparkling air, the breath
Of Titania combing the early night for
Elves and sprites that may be able
To speak for owls or perhaps blade worms
Challenging our perceptions of mornings
Perfect with coffee and lovemaking.

We change too much as we think:
"I will be witness." You will

Agree with me that we see in black.
We open the way we understand,
Relate. The world recedes, shrinks
And we are able to say, twisted
We play. Things cease. We open
The rooms up to allow more light.

We regard one another. We recognize
One another. The weather is a good
Topic to end this as we adopt
All information as special, except for the
Part about the nature of flash over.

THE HARP IN THE CIRCLE

The hard songs come through
Holes in the night sky,
An impending electricity of purpose
Gathers into patterns, constellations
Remembered from dares we took
As children, stories around
The night time fires,
The stars, reminders of our bone
Dust congealed within our sorry bodies.

Touched with grace for a moment,
they are able to form a mouth,
then a music, then a welter of instruments.

We hear them as animal voices,
Frogs and loons, crow talk,
The coughing of a cat,
Slap of fish on quiet water.

Oh let us sing the hard songs.
Songs of goodbye and of parting,
Of winds on the moors and
Mists moving across bogs
where plants eat meat,
Dreaming they are gods,
Where love flees a room
Dense with violins and clarinet
Laments. Pieces of loves across
Ages of time, dead ancestors
And friends turn from our embrace
To ride the night sky forever,
To pour through shining holes in the night sky.

VISITATION BY MIRACLES

A night train grinds
The edges of our understanding.

We make light of it, thinking
It is only a small disturbance,
Something we can overcome,
A brightness there in that late occurrence.

We are given to know many things.
Why I cry being so much different
Than why you cry and how would
We know what fills the heart or leaves
It open for visitations by miracles.

Somewhere it comes together, where
The tracks seem to converge in a distance.
But that is a place we cannot reach
Given all things from sleep and dreams,
To heated arguments and cursing at one another.

Eventually the sounds recede, a long
Hollow road into a further darkness.
We essay to bring songs, some kind of gift
To it. It remains an unknown god,
A blistering of angels just before consciousness
Decides we have had enough and leaves.

PICTURES OF PEOPLE MAKING LOVE

I was looking at some pictures
Of people making love and I wondered
Who they were this morning.
If they had walked along the cliff
Edge near the beach to watch the morning
Ease itself across the water? Did
They smell the seaweed? Did they
Listen to the wave sounds and the
Fog horns unanswered song as they talked
So beautifully you'd think the
Walls of heaven were being described,
Just by the way they were talking
To each other? Was it the sea
That made them remove their
Clothing and wander into each
Other, wonder into each other
'Caravans spilling out of their thighs'
And the bones singing of the lovely
Flesh touching like this so
That they wanted to keep some part
In pictures and they did they had
Their talk and were as leaves
And were as faith is so we are told,
So they could return to these images
Wondering who they were then and what
Happened and why did it all look
Like this and who else would see
Them here and float away on the
Images watching the sunlight on
The flesh, the bells of their bodies
Making that sound full of hurrah
And the waves coming back into focus
After a long time? The apple tree
Still in the background, the wonder
Piling up like forests against the sea.
Where is paradise now with its glory,
Its truth, the flames that are their
Flesh, the nobility that lives above
And shines incomparably on all human beings?

LE MAL DU PAYS

We find evening wandering among
The trees of the park: taking
His name slowly from the late
Afternoon as she slips into
Shadow, stretching a bit, easing
Her language of birds and insect sounds
Toward evening, offering them as gifts.

Lights begin to blink on
Across the valley. From here
They could be angels who, having
Heard the vespers bell, hurry
So not to be late for the last hour.

We can want no more than
To be here together, a witness.
Perhaps it is only that we have
Chanced to find ourselves surrounded
By the hour that moves this feeling
Through us and into the landscape.

Perhaps it is a knowledge of something
We had not anticipated understanding
Quite yet and so are still unable to
Name it properly that does this.

We stand together here a long
Time. Finally it becomes so dark
I can no longer see you clearly.
Stars begin to blow across the sky.

THE LOGOGRIPHS

A bundle of harps
Designated by a quiet
Dialect not spoken in this
Province but having the music
Within it that drives the
Labial tones of the flute
From its strings.

Some would call it magic,
The tone bending the meaning
Of gestures and objects to
Tell a completely different
Fact concerning the way
One wishes for something
Unattainable, evoking
A great longing both
Attractive and repellent
In its phantasm of music
Making. We never understand it.
Still we never fail to listen.

LEAVING THE MOUNTAIN

We will leave this one on the mountain.
There is a crystal stillness that permeates
These high places. The dark hands cannot
Do their blood wonders here.

The delights of the heavens are invented
Here. We can abandon the pain for a moment.
It will find some creature to orchestrate
Itself into a beautiful goddess and show it
To us.

"Oh my dear, so this 'Is what goes on here."

The darkness moving away

From the garden, the wheel, the hunger,
The distress of the spirit finally has a place
Where it can mount the golden back of the deer.
And the deer will sing to it...

"lullla, lullay,
Can you hear, Can you hear?"
As it was

In the beginning, is now, and ever shall be.

And I think about the fires leaping from
The fingers, the fires turning the wheels
As they breathe the same air we breathe,
World without end and the rudder
Grows loud in the empty sea and we
Find it unusual that the muscles of God
Carry us so lightly across the slouching world.

FALLING INTO THE FIELD OF TIME

From the edge of the boat
We could see the stars
Reflected in the water. We knew the
Many names of the moon and sang
To the fishes there below, the ones
Who swallowed stars and dreamed
The night sky beneath the sea.
The fish believe we are their rapture
As we sing. We believe the fish
To be gems of priceless value,
Wandering through the mind,
Bearing the names of the seas.

That night we slept on deck
Listening to the wind and waves
Tell stories of fire on
Islands so far away that one
Can but learn their names,
To visit these places is simply
Not possible in a single lifetime.

When dawn came we could no longer
Tell if we were male or female.
Deer gather at our feet. We
Feed them from bowls. We see
Death with its flocks of birds
Wheel and circle overhead.
We decide to make music forever.
We dance and sail on.

3. CHILD'S MOON

CHILD'S MOON

This is a child's moon.
It is that yellow, crooked
And obviously wants someone
To play with, anyone would suffice.

Here it is above this written landscape
With ascending letters playing the part
Of buildings and the windows of other letters
Allowing an entire city to be built
Below it, making a small night in a village.

When we can't remember names
Any longer and only the sweetness
Of faces comes through the door
Of the soul, tossing their light around,
Let us remember this child's moon
With its big eye and bright smile

Glowering upon us, trying to be serious
About it all and knowing we have
No way to explain that we would have
This evening no other way than how
It now appears, throw in a few more stars.

HISTORY

We thought then, when we were traveling,
The children knew something
Special, the way the light moved in their eyes,
The kinds of sounds they chose to become
Words. We would watch the owls
Bearing gifts of curious silver on silent
Wings. Not one of us said a thing.

I supposed that all things were
Like this. The rising of the moon
Was on everyone's lips. How wonderful.
How pale. We had never seen a moon
Such as this one. Each time it was new.

Now, standing on the high places near
The edge of the water, we think the wind
Has something important to say. It does
Not. It speaks but it has no words. It is
Tongue for the trees who tell us of
Bees, the names of the seasons,
The kind and number of the breezes,
How light makes sound through the cambium.

We have been so often wrong that for a
Moment we doubt the children.

We discover a red color we have
Never seen before. Language
Abandons us just before dusk.
We question each other with gestures,
Frantic to recall how it was
We made fire, how we knew to use
These roads, where we had been.

I HAD A PLAN LIKE EVENING

I had a plan like evening.
The stars were a soft red velvet.
Someone had picked the moon,

Kept it written on a small piece
Of paper I kept in my back pocket,
Even washed it twice, but it was good.

I could pick it up anywhere and dance
To it and everyone would be surprised,
Like someone knowing your name after
Not seeing them for many years.

Someday I will tell you all about it.
We will sit by the edge of the morning
Whispering about everything, afraid to wake
The day but wanting to do so badly.

There is a rapture that comes
Just in speaking of treasured things,
That wants them to be memories,
That wants them held in the mind
Until time comes for its claim.
We need be fully present to notice them.

Maybe if we stand here on the edge of this
High place and reach up as if to touch it all?

FINDING THE OLD LANGUAGE

In a rage to know all things,
Or as many things as it is possible
To know when one is eleven years old.

The divine walking amongst
Our friends, choosing this one
And that one, taking them away.

Unlacing their memories,
Giving their recognition of others
To the winds, to the birds,
Both flying away in a flurry of noise.

Electrical storms across the brain
At any time; just sitting there,
Getting out of bed, walking from one
Room to another.

All that was familiar
Suddenly not at all
Understandable.

Time without borders.
Anything could happen
At any instant,
Or perhaps not happen at all.

Waking from a summer nap.
The light, enchanting, over everything,
Temperature and sound engaged
In a magnificence of waking.
The world, yes!

Rulers of the mind,
All chemicals and fires
In the neurons and synapses.

More and more information
Beyond explanation.
The half-remarkable question:
"What is it that we are part of,
And what is it that we are?"

The delight of the dance,
The endless business of water.
That which is love,
Beneath the stars,
Inside all of sleeping,
Surrounded by its
Insistence on forever

Waking once again in the same
Room. Still here upon the Earth.
Doing things that become familiar,
To us. No longer surprised
By every act, by each event.

Moving through the day,
Learning laughter and
Helping one another to
Understand how something
Works. Finding the old
Language, the color, the
Limited means of expression.

IF THERE IS NOWHERE

If there is nowhere for the spirit
To move, it builds its house in that
Place. We find wonder in the way
Distance reveals objects on the edge
Of disappearing. We find names for the way
A hand opens.
We give special attention
To the gestures trees make. "They are
Caressing the air," we say.
There is a story, seldom told, of seeing
And not seeing, more than opening and
Closing the eyes.
We say dreaming is a way
Of seeing. We call from our sleep to
The waking world. It is a place
Where sound neglects language and
Spills from the lips, unhinged. It
Is unseen, a particle of the night.
What is seen: a body writhing beneath
Sheets—an avalanche of form.

A SLIGHT BREATHING

Hovering over the words,
Herding them, moving them
Into small groups. Full of meaning.

Here, the description of the heavens
Staggers forward, dragging
Its collection of constellations
Behind it; fully aware
That these pictures are but part
Of light seen from a single
Place, struggling to maintain
Themselves as the heavens
Reel around them.

These, are the words of lovers.
There is no end to them.
They slide and describe,
Word after word, the varieties of touch;
Definite descriptions, of flesh
Meeting flesh, in all temperatures and climates.

Gratefully, we follow these things,
Charmed that language
Allows us such rooms,
Such variety of discourse.

From the dark hills comes
The coughing of lions,
Calls of birds. William
Blake, moving room to room
Searching for the right phrase.

SACRED HARP MUSIC

The language off on its own
Dance. sometimes, when the night
Spreads itself like a lover across
The bed of dreaming I can smell
The musk of words on my skin.
A way of saying that cannot
Be made with the mouth.
I run my tongue along the lips
of this lover. It is exquisite
as in bone pain or heartbreak.
When words touch this deep
There are flaming swords, there
Over east of Eden. One cannot determine
Depth of feeling. There is no device
To measure this deep.
Light cannot penetrate here,
Only the movements of breath
In and out, in and out, words
Themselves are not admitted here.
Still, it is language, still it is
Touching that drives so deep
Into the core of loving that
Everything is understood.
It is such of mystery that no one
Has blood enough or time to
Offer explanation. Amazing grace.
How the mountains rise from the plain.
How the seas rush to know all
That is called land.

QUICKNESS

We will hardly notice when this
Is over. A sudden flurry of description
As if a poem were an uncommon species
Of bird that hardly ever visits these
Colder climates, even during the short
Summer days when insects form dense
Clouds in the air and conspire to
Be the noise filling the night. Clouds of them
Blocking sunlight and even the moon
For moments at a time and then
There they are shining again against
The buzzing darkness with its curious

Movement, wings through the thickness
Of the air. The ground littered
With hundreds of thousands of
Tiny winged bodies in the morning
Just as new clouds begin to
Form close to the surface of the lake,
Fish rising through rainbows to snap at them.

A KIND OF SINGING

The light beginning to crackle and glow
Around the buildings on the horizon.
In traveling through this place
We have no idea why such a phenomena
Should occur. It's rather like a
Small child being born and immediately
Becoming recognized as a great king.
What are the chances of such a thing?

The evening scoots down the low hills
As if it were another child, on a slide,
Being called to dinner just as he
Finally gains his spot at the top.
What to do? Come home now?

Sit down, press one's legs into the
Sides of the slide and take as much
Time as possible to descend to the ground.
Everyone will understand somehow.

When we reach the bottom of the hill,
The entire landscape looks embossed;
A storybook cover one could run one's
Hand over and still feel the real worth
The story has to hold. No one has
Visited this place below the hill
For so long, we have forgotten the songs
That used to be sung about it.
We believe we are making up a new song.

CEREMONY

So many voices. A chorus
Speaking together. There is
Grace in the way the words
Form here. We have no idea
What is being said. But there

It is, pure and outlandish
As late June with its
Dreams of water and Summer
Love caught in its loins.

We walk along the sidewalks
On the edges of the park.
The fireflies are just starting
To be seen so we sit and wait
For the dark to consume everything.

I am in love with you, you
The one reading this. I want to
Take you in my arms and touch
You intimately, make love with you
With great ceremony and unbridled lust,
To be a chorus within you, not
Singing at all, but speaking so we
May hear in our core, abandoning gender,
Fine and carnal, pleading another kind
Of Summer, another mouth upon yours
Where speech stops attending us
Where all becomes sensation,
Steam rising from the ocean surface
Even before dawn is aware of it.

4. THE PERFECT OFFERING

TIGER WAND
for Joseph Raffael

Frog sounds
in the early morning.
They have voices, move
together to form a great
voice, voice, in the air
we who listen, those who
care, lifting like the spirit
departing the body wearing
six colors and forming
an attitude of giving
with the hands. All this
falling, lifting me
up from the morning coffee
wiping the sleep from my face,
listening to the frogs
and thinking they are other
voices, children moving
in their dreams, those who
don't come back from sleep
tonight, the breath of a lover
moving in my ears, departing.

'THERE IS NO LANGUAGE WITHOUT DECEIT'
—Italo Calvino

The thing seen
And the seer are the
Same thing, yet neither
Knows it. The seer suspects
That this is so but the world
Denies the knowledge until
A particular time.

In the latter part of the day
Three men will appear with a bag
That seems too heavy for any
One man to carry. They will offer
It for sale and will produce
Lovely tales of the contents
Of this bag.

There is a holy light that descends
Near here just before the sun
Forgets itself and slips below
The horizon as if it were about
To hide something from us.
Here we will gather. Many will
Make fires and begin to speak
Tales that at first seem ordinary
But eventually become punctuated
With giraffes and birds of strange
Plumage, alleys where the eyes
Of great cats glow and one can
Hear dice clatter to the cobble
Stones or see doorways open for
A second and a beautiful woman may
Be seen laughing invitingly, then
Disappearing behind the door bringing
A pointed kind of darkness that
Stills the voices of the story tellers
For a moment.

Tea is made and occasionally a harp
Or flute can be heard nearby making
A melody that we feel we have always
Known and wish to tell others about.

The clicking of shoes against the stones,
Small sounds that might be language
Engage us and we begin to feel
That this is truly correct.

UNABLE TO EXPLAIN

We sat on the edge of the blue
Inlet and listened for the question
To become complete. A slight
Drift of smoke carried the scent
Of the cities through our clothing,
Peeling layer after layer of feeling
From us as if it were the heart,
Caught in its room of ribs and breathing,
Unable to understand hands, the movements
Of high mountain goats among the pinnacles of forgetting.

Sounds poured forth from us,
Continents of them, ripe and with
A million yellow mouths, all wanting
Something other than words could
Give, caught in melody and stripped
Before our eyes of the darling vestments
So beloved by men everywhere;
Truth, Knowing, the Sublime, Instinct.
"All lost, lost," the captain said, unable
To recognize the land any longer.

We have no maps for things like this.
We are forever thinking we know
What will happen. We are forever
Calling, searching for echoes, the voice of angels,
The smiles of children blessed with tenderness,
Founded in waking up to see the sun
Slipping between the window blinds,
Not a dream at all, rather a way of knowing.
We embrace them and weep endlessly.
We name ourselves rain forest.

THE RAIN

The rain is talking to the back door.
"Pat, pat, pat", it says, not even listening to itself.
You are coming down the wind, naming
The clouds as you do. The sidewalks reflect
Your footsteps, "pat, pat, pat", like an old
French song fashioned of late summer and
A piano in a room overlooking the Mediterranean.

Under the leaves of the trees birds huddle
Remarking at how much you look like the rain.
Their badinage is marvelous. They have eighty
Three different tones for describing the way rain
Looks as it falls upon water, the sea, ponds, lakes,
the rivers, brooks. There is not one that describes
Your coming down the wind. They explode in
Welters of birdsong and squabbling.

All day the sun has refused to look through
The clouds. It had decided to leave the day to
Ducks, swans and the dreams of fish gazing
Toward the sky at the spreading circles of the raindrops,
As if they were a ceiling of water kissing water.
Now it has heard you upon the wind and looks
Through the trees. For a moment the air is draped
In diamonds. They cover you as you roll across
The back of the wind. The air itself inhales.

The rain listens to itself, searching madly for
A language, "Pat, pat, pat", it says, "Look
Past the wind, look past the wind." I do.

TALKING TO A GREAT BIRD

When we reached camp two on the North
Face of the mountain we came across the nesting
Site of a great bird. Larger than any bird previously
Encountered, similar to a crow but as big as a two
Story building with a beak as yellow as candy corn,
A voice that hissed as it came across his tongue.

It was old but quite virile. It had a mate living in
Another remote part of the world. It is remarkable
That no one had encountered these birds previously.

"What is even possible?" said the bird in an agitated manner.
"How large is the evening after all?" "It depends on where
You are when the evening is with you." "I am only as
Big as your imagination will allow me to be. There are
People looking at this right now and figuring you for a liar,
At least a spinner of tales. They will find no reality in
Anything you say. On the other hand, I do exist and
My beak is large enough to end the controversy.

I shall be seen in the distance only until such a time
That one needs to see me as I am, indeed as
All the others on this wandering earth are seen.

It is of no import that I should be perceived as large
Or small or that I am like the Dodo or the passenger pigeon.
I am here or I am not here. Your fancy will Waltz you
To Vienna in less than five minutes. Let me stop talking."

A SWEET WHISPER

A sweet whisper clipping the tops of waves.
The humidity changing the colors to pastels,
Opening my eyes in already late morning.

I can hear the birds arguing in the palm
Trees. It seems they have important things
To do. They abandon the yard.

I am working over the lyrics to a song
I can barely remember. It says that heartbreak
Can be overcome if one stops feeling.

I am amazed at the way afternoon
Lopes into the room, recognizing everything
But how my heart understands distance.

I begin to sing my own song. There is a
Moment where everything that prompted it
Becomes real again. I can hardly continue.
The birds return and gather near my windows,
Silent except for their beaks tapping the glass.

THE PERFECT OFFERING

Somehow it always escapes me.
I find myself driving home, suddenly
Remembering that the perfect offering
Had been made and I had been dreaming
Or was distracted by divine light coming
Through the glass and playing on the floor.

Fortunately I have the luxury of seeing
Fields of vineyards and a brown or
Slate gray river near me reminding me
That it is okay if the perfect offering
Has eluded me once again.

This is how prayer works. The words
May never come without the soul feeling
Slightly embarrassed or unable to compose
Itself clearly. A limited means
Of expression to be sure, but a good
One. The afternoon undoes the day
And its bodice is more than alluring,
It is devastating and hugely erotic
With notions I can't even associate
With my own body, like kissing
Strangers fully on the mouth and believing
They will be my lovers and I shall
Be theirs no matter what the circumstances.

We will drive home in the late afternoon
Marveling at the sun and the quality
Of the light. We will speak to one another.
There will be deep music in every single word.

ONE HUNDRED POEMS

The way light eats the horizon.
The way Japanese ghosts
Have no feet. Birds gather
In the trees. They say things
To each other that we can hear
But are unable to understand.
A glass reflects the rising
Of the moon. Reading secret
Messages in the pattern of leaves
Upon the ground. There were
Pieces of conversation stuck to
His teeth. A great cultus of
Admonition flourished around
Any mention of the present tense.
The rafters of language are draped
With banners showing the most
Intimate secrets of the verb.
Landscape is spoken of only
In regard to feelings. There is
No middle distance. It becomes
Inevitable that dense conversation
Cover the face of the moon,
That night untie itself
From any reason and reduce
All poetry to whispers which
Remind one of the wind.
One hundred poems are written
At exactly the same moment.
They are mistaken for the oceans,
Are fished and thought of great
Depth. One crosses them
Full of wonder, lingering as long
As possible to watch
The waves, the shadow
Flight of birds across
Their sweet surface.

BUILDING

Open your mouth. I will open my mouth.
There will be words. They will play
Upon the teeth and thread themselves
Into the splendor that was our
Living body, our hearts so in love, our gaze.
The objects hardest to break remain.

We keep waiting for the gaze to come.
It has traveled a long way now
And finds solace in the scent of cinnamon,
Any gestures that sparkle like gems
As they unravel and become fragments.

*

I broke the front
while going up
and what
came before
was thorn
on cheek
from across
the bay
to pull a tear
from both my eyes

My thoughts are surprised
To find they have become
Crows overnight and leave
In dark flocks squawking
Loudly, confused at what once
Was a lovely pastoral
Landscape, searching for food.

We've come to take you home,
Rife with the cast off
Carapaces of ten thousand

Prophecies, the husks of as many
Songs, the fragile wings of dragonflies
And persistent banging
Against the doors of heaven.
Clouds of black mosquitos
Sizzle around us,
A music filled with
Borrowed blood built
On the edge of a perfection
Of chance and persistent hope
Huddled together in curious embrace.

Leave us now.
We are no longer afraid.
The way is crisp with moonlight.
The dogs are anxious for the hunt.
Taste has made our mouths unreasonable.
We will cross the mountains
We understand the promises.
We accept this way of communicating.

When all is accomplished
We too will be transfigured.
You will see the purity of our intentions
And hail us as true instruments
Of conscious news unleashed on the most
Trying of times, not content with the ordinary
And willing to auction
Everything you have read
For the warm jets truth
Will bring to our visions.

I will bring you a cloak made of days.
All their weather and possibilities.
It will be our church.
Pray for us.

THE PERFECT BALANCE OF THE SPIRAL

I started out to tell you something,
Something of the morning, the exclamations
Birds orchestrate as marks of color
Against the insistence light makes
Upon us as we move slowly away
From sleep and into the crisp
Air of Autumn before everyone
Is awake and we can sit for a moment
As the day establishes itself in our
Minds as something substantial but untouchable.

But I got lost turning around and
Around on the lawns far from
The house, eyes open, seeing that
Small grove of trees, then the
Lane toward the house, the creek,
Its stone bridge, the two hills
With the folly upon the higher one
Trying to find a classical landscape
This close to the city, finally,
The house itself with the window
Glass looking golden and unreal
As I reeled round and round.

Perhaps a song would help here
But the whole thing will not stop
Turning and the earth itself knows
that and continues to throw up
Wonder upon wonder into our being
Here in early October. It has its
Own music. The birds still sing
In the nighttime and we have a piece
Of the whitest moon to take to
Our beds as we move through the
Picture galleries and the night views
Of the fountains from the second
Floor toward the garden.
We hear string music come from afar.

Closing our eyes for a moment
We find the balance once again,
The bowing to each other, the delicious
Fragility of the dance.

DIMENSIONS OF
THE MORNING

SEVERAL KINGS

Several kings are sitting
watching the death change
enter the eyes of a young
saint who has fallen from
a small hole in the sky.

He wears a brightly feathered
arrow midway between his shoulders
and his head. One of his eyes
is slightly glazed, as from a fire.
He is very quietly not breathing.

The kings squat closer and shuffle
their feet. Little puffs of dust
do a war around them.

They watch the saint to see
if he is going to move.
One of the kings touches the
glazed eye with his finger.

They get on their horses and ride
away. None of them has spoken yet.

NOTHING COMING

Someone sprung up in a field
head of silver, eyes like ours
and I am sorry to have fallen here.

Didn't any of you see your god.
Didn't he stand before you with
his eyes open and write long books
while he was warm and his mouth
rested on yours.

Or is it that you don't know me?
It is that you have never spoken
to one who is on fire? Do you
think me too clean a thing to
speak to you, you surround me with guns
aim your pretty cannons at my tree
cursing and dark?

I can say no name to you.
I have apparently come to the wrong
earth. I have heard that every man
was light and beauty. This is darkness
endless darkness and brothers are falling
beneath what you call heaven.

What you call heaven is going to fall
in on you and kill today and you
won't even know it because the halls you
call life are so damn empty everything
smells like death to you.

I am so unnatural I feel like God.

THEY ARE GOLDEN

They are golden.

They are near.

They watch us.

The fine silk of their thoughts
move upon us like old songs
and we are seen together
dancing in the fields, children
of the same sun.
Occasionally
they reach down with their hands
and clumsily lift one or another
of the dancers to them; look
into their eyes sorrowfully and
finally place them down amazed
at their shiny toys.

This lifting and setting down
measured in days and years
or from one true kiss to another.

You blind fool.
This you call death?

IT IS MORNING

It is morning.
The heavy eye of the moon
lies in a tangled heap
just above a small clump
of trees. There is no movement
anywhere in the land.

A mist begins rising.
A mist that just fits inside
the shirt of a man, near the
narrow space of heart and lungs.

Now some bullets are walking
in the air. They are about
the size and shape of bees.
One of them has entered
the mist. The others follow.

Quickly they eat the narrow
space inside there shirt.

It is morning.

**"It is difficult to draw away from the face of God - it is like
a warm fire, it is like dear sleep, it is like a great anthem;
yet there is a stillness all about it, a stillness full of lights."**
...Lord Dunsany

We watched them from our towers
and they sparkled like a first morning,
their hands held perfumes of deepest
rose and their eyes were full of
the sound of birds in jasmine.
Extending their cool hands to ourselves
they bade us come in, 'come in.'

Crossing the room he saw three flowers
dangling from a broken vase. Someone
had left them for him to see. He was
sure. It was morning outside and he
looked past the flowers, the disordered room,
and there were small animals playing in the snow.
They tore at each other with tiny teeth and
became red on the snow. Whispering.

The game was too old. He reloaded his gun
and sat down. Eventually they would come and he
would be ready for them. It had been many years.

The sun set.

"You are like a maiden who is sleeping." The
voices walked round him and the night wore its
long coat and walked quietly on the hills.
"You are like a wanderer from Kyfouth and your
shoes show the desert in a perfection of sand.

He moved.

The guns came up and spilt their terrible seed
upon him. He moved and the dream went deeper.
There were paths filled with things he did not know,
like Christmas. He became himself and the snow

showed a small group of men, with hands like dogs
running in tight file across a field. Even then
he didn't stir or wipe the redness from his eyes.
A fine lady with night wound in her hair
bent close to him and said words in his ear.

"What is that way?' he said half-rising.

"The changing of the seasons" someone answered.
"I am moving then?"
"Yes."

Outside the small animals had slowly moved away,
crying softly and licking their soft bodies.

OH SAVAGE WONDER

Oh, savage wonder in this kingdom.
The long armed maidens offer their guns
and eyes to a night god and everything comes
running through the front door, just like
the blues.

And it has a cart.
And it has small hands that fit tight
around your throat when you think everything has already
broken down.
and it plays merry songs as the wheels of flame
find their own vineyards and melt away into a face
you knew as your own.

We entered the town later in the evening.
The lights had just come on and small groups
of people had gathered around their tables
eating and laughing together. We were very cold.

The soldiers had come there ahead of us and some
of the houses were still smoking. I held her hand
much tighter than I should have and she spoke.

"Is something wrong?" she asked. Her eyes were like
baby suns and warmer. "No, it is nothing, I was just
thinking it must have been like this before we went to
sleep in Marlee." She seemed satisfied and followed
fairly close behind me.

We reached the last street. In another few minutes
we would be back in the forest and quite safe from
everything. I turned to tell her and she was gone.

From the other end of the street I could see a small
band of men with dogs heading my way. They were looking
for something. I sat down on a stone step and waited
for them to catch up with me.

AND HE SAID

and he said:

leaning foreword over the table
looking hard at his friends face

"Do you hear me Al, do you hear...
it was 1965, in Cleveland, before
the revolution...yes before...

and Hallister hears and looks hard
across the table.

    And from outside the window
    the ground catches three horsemen
    coming up the dirt road, horses
    flaming with dust and winter sun.

    They are grinning like old pirate
    movies and being thirteen and the
    sound of the night moving like
    a police siren in his blood.

    He looks harder and some old
    leaves blow the thin snow up
    and across the room, filling
    his voice with warm and rooms
        of imagined legs.

"They were singing Al, singing as I lifted
my head and saw the sun on the streets and
everyone was alive and cars were all over the
streets and the wine and on .25 a glass or
somedays cheaper..."

    And from inside they slowed down
    like locomotive wheels hissing and
    scraping against steel legs, finally
    stopping...chests heaving and far away
    the riders were dancing and some people

they had never known were standing in the middle
of a large rock, talking and they could
not hear a word any of them were saying, two
men and one lady, she with ruffled dress and
the smell of castles in her long hair.

THE MILLION EYES OF THE GRASS

are staring at you.
You cannot lie down upon their
Faces and escape their gaze of fire.

All the killing of yourselves come
streaking home in their arms. The
soft lips they touch you with are sorry
poisons for all of you. They feel the
steel teeth cutting into them and give
way remembering the conservation of energy,
remembering they shall someday toss and laugh
above your body.

Once a child walked along a stream.

Once a tiger hid in the tall grass and
slept away from everyone.

Once two common soldiers waited forever
for the sun to come up and find them lost.

Once a man with dark hands washed himself
in the stream nearby and dried those hands
on thick reeds.

Once a farmer walked for hours watching
the wheat plot and turn, and ran home screaming.

Once an old man spoke to the sky and the grass
answered. He felt this was right.

Go away for awhile and the grass grows high.
It covers the ground and green and brown and
its soul is weeds and its heart is a yellow
butterfly on a summer.

Go away for awhile and the snow finally covers
it. We don't know what the snow and the grass
say to one another. They speak for months in white
tongues and the air is filled with the voce of snow.

We know in spring the ground rends and cracks
and the streams run full and the grass rises
and looks at us safe in our cities. Its tiny
eyes pushing up in sidewalks and near old trees.

Father trees, protect us from the grass that burns and the
grass that is older than yourself. See into its heart and
tell it we are men, how pitifully the trees look down.
How godlike the heavens of grass look up into our eyes.

RIVERS OUT

She was thinking about the sky again.
All the sky things: clouds, tall horses
with silver manes and breath the temper
of all winds, stars and their small brothers,
rain and its sister sea, jewels and the
hopes of endless halls, of fish in them.

She thought the sky around and the spirits
of earth came to her, colored robes whirling,
speaking strange tongues and fishing out the sky
with questions of themselves, clicking and hammering
like typewriters, like men in the streets tearing
holes, like gunbursts that slam into the page
and die there, never showing their ugly faces
to man as more than words.

The sky changed, the robes descended and
long rain, the time of unrest, the gathering
of ways to one way began and she was sea
in herself, her many arms depending.

SOMEDAYS

Somedays it seems like it isn't
important to say anything
to anybody,
but then you do and
things get better.

Once was a small king
who ate nothing but celery
and was always mad..

Stars were spiders
and spiders were stars
to him. Somebody told him
that and he believed it
fully.

When the stars came out
at night he would hold
his baby tight and the
light that was them
would shine on you.

You see what I mean
somedays it's like that
and everything is still
alight.

MY EYES HAVE SEEN THE GLORY
OF THE OPENING OF THE

door. The cat strolled in the door on its hind legs.
Held tightly in its paws was a small revolver, hammer
pulled back, safety off.

"Hello sucker, said the cat. "I'm here to take you out
of this life, the angel of death as it were, and this gun
will do it. Will do it quick, will do it clean."

I was surprised. How could I tell my friends about this one.
Certainly a hallucination of some kind. A cat with a gun.
"But why and who? And why a cat?"

"Why not a cat, he said leaning against the wall.
Life is like that, you never know what's going to happen
next. One minute just sitting there typing and then WHAM!
In I stroll and the whole book changes. Simple stuff man,
so simple you forget it."

"Who sent you?"

"Uh uh, no reasons. You know better than that. Things
just happen. No reasons. You think up the reasons later,
it makes the time go together better, that's all."

"Would you like a bowl of milk cat?" I asked.

"Sure", he said and laid the gun down. "Sure I'd like a
bowl of milk."

He walked on all fours over to the milk and began drinking.
I quickly picked up the gun and put it high on a shelf.

"Were you really going to kill me?" I asked the cat.

The cat lapped its milk, the later afternoon sun did a dance
across its long fur. He looked up at me and squinted, made
a cat noise.

Some days, I said to myself, somedays it gets so real.
Cats with guns and poems with people inside of them.
What next, I said and the room was very, very quiet.

THE ROOM RETURNING

The ladder stretched from the bed
to the floor, maybe only two feet
or maybe forever. He touched the rope
rungs and descended like autumn into
beyond the floor, the room giving up
around the edges and finally quitting
after an hour or so.

One floor, another, the seasons like
mad bees or animals with chains around
their necks broke loose and raced toward
him, gnashing and frothing. He descended like
the holy ghost, everything was a metaphor.

The last rung.

The floor again only two feet away, feeling
foolish he stepped down and knew it was wrong.

The smell of eggs and bacon, coffee bubbling
 its morning song. Touching the top of the
dresser he was six years old again. The kitchen
was someone else's and a mother was telling
him "morning honey." He raced back into the
bedroom, the ladder being drawn up slowly
to the top of the bed and far above the room,
so high he was forgetting faster than possible
his young wife sleeping there. Oh God, oh God!

IT'S KIND OF WHAT DEATH IS LIKE

There was a young girl standing just
outside the door of the house where she lived
watching some ducks swimming around. They
were pretty. Some of them made noise.

Suddenly a tree that stood far around the edge
of the duck pond lifted itself off the ground
and started moving around the edge of the water
to where she was. Its roots carrying
it faster and faster.

The ducks in their small minds saw the sun move,
saw the shade toss its head, and they squawked and
swam to hide from things gone mad.

The young girl smiled and took a step backward.
The tree moved on toward the girl.
The ducks squawked and swam round and round.
The girl moved backward. The pond spilled toward her.
The sun swirled and mixed in leaves and feathers,
in water and doorways, and just when everything was
going its fastest, I slid into a chair, stuck a piece
of paper into my machine and slowed the whole thing
down just to see how it looked.

IT'S LIKE A SUN IN THE STOMACH

It's like a sun in the stomach.
You were sitting on the edge of the bed
and there was a smile growing out of your face
like you had just hit on the most wonderful thing
in the world and it was all of us.

It's like a broken cookie in the bottom of an ashtray.
You are standing on the edge of a large fish pond.
There were some ducks swimming around and the wind
was blowing. You shoved your hands down inside
your pockets and everything looked like a black and white
photograph of somebody standing next to a pond.

It's like the sound of a motor running or a train wobbling
along a track just on the edge of hearing. Somewhere
closer a radio starts up and is turned down very quickly.

It's like candy bar wrappers in the gutter.
It's like your pillow in the dark.
It's like everyone in the house asleep except you.
It's like hearing water run in the morning.
It's like horses grazing on the tops of hills.
It's like finding nothing on the beach except rocks.
It's like a glass that just broke and the pieces are still
wobbling.

If you go back to sleep be sure and tell me.
The spaces in between my life where nothing too much
happens and I always forget to write it all down.

A HAND OPENS

A hand opens. It contains a beautiful sign.
The sign says: "Behold the Beautiful."

I still think about that.

AND HE OPENED HIS MOUTH

And he opened his mouth
and his lips moved and
I saw his tongue working
against his teeth and lips
my ears strung out listening
to a great humming like all
the beehives in all the small
rooms played into each other
and above this his voice an
open hand high and clear as
the first night with rain
alone came swimming the words
forgot and smiles like clover
fields a-roaming in the gloaming
the hands of song came into
me and the whole horn section
stood up and played their riff

lights blinking on and off
down the road a way.
"Let's get away from this place
doll"
"Okay big boy, you show the way."

furs and bees and wide brim hats
It's all in how you make it scat.

dei - da dee.

THE RETURN OF THE QUEEN TO KEN-NI

She came down the road, she came
and in her eyes were storms from the wild things
and her voice shook like a drunken wind.

She spoke to children gathered in the roads
and they burst into small fires for the sun
was in them. They caught at her arm and she
fed them streets and darkness and the banging
of harps made of clear silk and made of blue stone.

She went from the towns and her breath was the
ground
and the earth was alive with the crawling things.
The long trains of her hair was moved in the trees
and the sky too with arrows and ducks,
dressed and with teeth, she saw them driving
down into her arms and the ponds shook, offering
white fish, the plants of the brooks brimmed yellow
with clouds, driving the dust around her.

*
**

And all the while, the while, the long time,
a silver piano with man attached, played its
green felt hammers against thin strings
singing on and on to some fabled eye.

ABOUT FLOWERS

There was a giant, do you hear lassie,
came down from the spring he did, out
of the winter and down the foggy slopes
to take him some sun back home.

And we watched, 'twas like a dream we watched
his ungainly hands reach up and take the smallest
part of the light down and wrap it in his shirt.

>   in the valley, valley oh
>   the town is rising up its
>   scythes and pitchforks, listening
>   from the fields to the bells going
>   mad and the sound of thousands of rats
>   running in the streets, to the sounds
>   they made oh the sounds.

Very quickly the giant walked down, lassie did
you hear, and laid his hands on the rocks and
pulled his huge self up over the highest cliff
in Marlee and he spoke out to the sea, across
the towns and their bells, across the hem of
dreams caught in the early morning air, he spoke
and his words moved the night from her mindless-
ness
and shook the turtles in the ponds and in one hand
he picked up his piece of sun and hurled it over
everything its bright throat bouncing off the waves
like a million fishes.

There was a giant, do you hear lassie
came down from the spring he did, out
of the dreams he came and the sun watched
him climb higher and higher until he was no
longer in sight.

WHERE HAVE YOU BEEN LATELY?

The gambler he rides a dark horse.
The gambler can't remember his name.
He's been living so long in the land of his mind
that his mind and his land are the same,

in the full moon
  the long gray arms of trees
   fold in gently and touch
  the smallest of lights in the forest

Inside the light an old man
with a peace of years inside
  moves across a room of leaves
  and train whistles, books and animals
  and looks out a small round
  window. Thinking.

    The sea unwinds itself upon a shore.
    The strung out watch of some god thing
    glistening like the back of a
    beautiful lady.

Softly, a rain begins falling.

slipping of leaves the moon
finding clouds. Warm air
holding us in kind suspenders
and the gambler takes the magic
cards from his pocket removes
the saddle from his horse
and reads by the campfire light.

END OF A CHILDREN'S STORY

And so there were
times when the little jade-
eyed man would sit in his
cardboard box and stare
for hours at the angels
who came and went before
the blind lady

and the lady became
everyday a bit more
clouded and her voice
would fail and fall off
into the months of the
year where sometime some
where someone had to be singing.

until one day the little
jade-eyed man put one foot
outside his box and found
that there was morning
just like the bird had said
it would be

dancing off into the pleasant
morning he waved at the angels
and sang all the songs she had
sung and gave all the birds
strange names so that they would
stay and wait for him.

Outside the box it was always
morning.

Then he was gone. The blind
lady picked up his box and
burned it. Then she went
into the house and went to
sleep. The jade-eyed man
had said he would return when
it was afternoon.

D.R. Wagner is the author of over thirty books and chapbooks of poetry and letters. He founded <u>press : today : niagara</u> & <u>Runcible Spoon</u> in the late 1960s and produced over fifty magazines and chapbooks. His work is much published and has appeared in many translations & anthologies. He is also a visual artist, producing miniature needle-made tapestries that have been exhibited internationally & are included in numerous publications & museum collections. He is, further, a professional musician, working as a singer-songwriter and playing guitar and keyboards. He taught Design at the University of California at Davis for over thirty years. He also taught in the Honors program at the university conducting classes in Poetry by Design. His most recent book is called *LOVE POEMS* from Cold River Press. D.R. currently resides in Locke, California the cultural center of the Sacramento River Delta.

COLOPHON

Toward Love & Selected Poems was designed and typeset by Bill Roberts in North Salem, New York. The text is set in Palatino which was designed by Hermann Zapf (1918—2015) in 1949. This typeface was noted for its beauty and increased legibility. This book is published in an open edition, of which 50 copies are numbered and signed by the author.

★ DRW ★
TLK